To Be a Man:
Johnnie Wilson, Jr.

Printed in USA
September, 2004
First edition, first printing
Book & cover design by Jerry Kelly
Printed by Printing Arts Press, Mt. Vernon, OH

Dedicated to my parents, Teddy and Olga Gluck, for teaching me
the importance of listening to stories, and to Johnnie Wilson Jr.,
for trusting me with his.

XOXOX
PRESS

Gambier, Ohio

see us at www.xoxoxpress.com
write us at xoxoxpress@yahoo.com

To Be a Man:
Johnnie Wilson, Jr.

An Oral History by
Susan Gluck Rothenberg

PRESS

❧

Because of the bias of white-dominated newspapers and the paucity of written records from representative Black sources, oral history is particularly important for revealing the identities and concerns of anonymous Negroes. It also permits a Black citizen to have a role in interpreting history.

Douglas Henry Daniels
Pioneer Urbanites—
A Social and Cultural History of San Francisco
(1980)

∽⚬

PROLOGUE

During the time I was working on this manuscript, an acquaintance asked, "What are you doing these days?" I told her that I was working on a book about the life of a 93-year-old man named Johnnie Wilson, expanding his oral history into a biography. Having never heard of Johnnie Wilson, she asked, "What was he famous for?"

I told her that there was no reason she should have heard of him and tried to briefly explain why his story was worth telling. But there was no way I could explain in a short conversation all that he had done with his life. Although given few opportunities, Mr. Wilson had not only used every opportunity offered, but created possibilities where none were obvious. Born in Louisiana early last century, an African-American in the deep South, Mr. Wilson moved beyond the real limitations placed on him by culture and time.

Johnnie Wilson is unknown to most of the world. Those who had the privilege of his companionship saw him as a man of honor who cared deeply for his family. They knew him to be a man to whom they could turn in times of need and one who willingly shared his love and life lessons. His story deserves to be told. Here it is, told in his own words, while the back-story of the book's creation is told in mine. I only hope this effort does justice to this extraordinary man.

S.G.R.
San Francisco
June 2004

INTRODUCTION

The driver and I began talking from the moment I got into the silver Lincoln on my way to the San Francisco Airport. At some point in our conversation, I mentioned that I was on my way to Santa Barbara to visit my daughter who had recently moved there after finishing college in Ohio. The driver and I began talking about the importance of family.

"You know," he said, "last Thanksgiving, we had five generations at our home for dinner. My grandfather was there, and my grandchildren were too. It sure was wonderful having everyone together."

Amazed to hear about five generations of one family being together, I asked how old his grandfather was.

"He's ninety-three," he said with pride. "He's really something. Still cooks, does woodworking, and boy-oh-boy, does he love baseball."

He went on to tell me more about his grandfather. As he spoke, his admiration and love for the older man were clear. The eldest of the five generations, his grandfather had been born early in the 20th century in Louisiana and had lived on a farm owned by his father. After the early death of his parents, he lived with his grandparents. As a young man, still in Louisiana, he played on a Negro baseball team and later moved to Galveston and then, during World War II, to San Francisco to work on the waterfront.

Impulsively, I asked if anyone had ever recorded his grandfather's stories. When he said no, I told him about my interest in oral histories and asked if he thought his grandfather would be willing to let me record his story. He thought he might, but suggested that "it would help if you knew something about baseball." I told him I thought I knew enough to get started.

At that time, using a car service for a trip to the airport was not my usual habit. In many ways, I think that my ride that particular morning was meant to be. When I asked the driver if his grandfather would talk to me, I almost looked over my shoulder to see who had asked the question. I was not usually that forward nor did I generally jump feet first into someone's life. Looking back, I am grateful that I did.

I was just completing work on a friend's oral history. Our two-year conversation had enabled my friend, Bill Lowenberg, to discuss his early life in Germany and Holland, as well as his experiences in five different concentration camps during the Holocaust. Bill had never previously shared his memories in depth. Telling his story had been a gift to himself, to his family and to me.

My interest in history, particularly the stories of individuals, has grown gradually. When I was seventeen, my grandfather told me about some of the cities he had visited before coming to the United States from Hungary. For some reason (probably adolescent self-absorption), I found it difficult to believe him. As I knew him, my grandfather was a tailor—a quiet man—and the adventurous young man of his stories didn't match the man sitting near me in the living room. I mentioned my doubt to my mother.

In her quiet way my mother said, "Grandpa did travel on his way here and even before. That's how he met Grandma. Instead of becoming a rabbi, Grandpa became a 'rabble rouser.' He traveled from town to town throughout Hungary and into other countries. When he came to Grandma's town, they met and married when she was sixteen." Rabble rouser? I was intrigued by the grandfather I didn't know, but despite my questions she wouldn't add more.

That summer I traveled to France with an aunt, uncle and cousins. I looked forward to asking my grandfather more about his youth when I got home, but he died while we were away. And though I've since learned more about his "rabble rousing," I regret not hearing his story in his own words and being able to read the emotion in his face. Hearing his story through the memories of others is not the same as hearing it first-hand and has sparked my desire to hear stories directly from their source. Bill gave me a gift in allowing me to help him tell his story to his family and friends. He let me be a part of sharing with his family a direct inheritance I wish I had received from my own relatives.

Following our airport ride, Lorrel Anderson, the driver of the car, spoke to his grandfather, Johnnie Wilson. Several weeks after the airport ride, Willie Mae Mackey, Johnnie Wilson's daughter, told me that if I wanted to come, her father would be happy to see me. We arranged a time to visit the following week, in March, 1997.

I drove to Mr. Wilson's home with some trepidation. Helping Bill record his story was one thing. Bill was a friend, someone I had known. Here I was going to see a total stranger. However, the stories Lorrel had shared intrigued me. Mr. Wilson's life spanned almost the whole century and as a black man in the United States, he had survived difficult times.

The small house in which Mr. Wilson lived with his daughter and son-in-law stands in a row of similar homes on a well-maintained block in the Bayview district of San Francisco. The Wilson-Mackey home is close to Candlestick Park, where the Forty-Niners play, as did the Giants before moving to their new ballpark. The house is also close to the old naval ship-yards at Hunter's Point.

Mrs. Mackey met me at the door over which hangs a sign that reads, "All of our guests bring happiness—some by coming; others by going." We went up the stairs and into the kitchen where Mr. Wilson was seated at the table by a window overlooking the street. The kitchen felt like the center of the home, a constant hub of activity. The small round table, next to a window, faces the street. Often, as Mr. Wilson described distance in his story, he would use something outside as a measuring point.

When I came into the room, Mr. Wilson stood to welcome me. He was six feet tall and had an amazingly straight stance, given his age. He wore wire-rimmed glasses and sported an English-style driving cap. I felt welcomed by his handshake and the warm smile on his very dark, rich, coffee-colored face. His smile and deep laugh came easily when he remembered something joyful.

After joining him at the table, I told him about my interest in helping record his life story. I showed him my small tape recorder and explained how I would tape, transcribe and edit his words, if he agreed. Almost immediately he said, "I'm ready," and started speaking before I could turn on the recorder. I quickly attached an auxiliary mike to his shirt, got the machine started, and our journey began.

As soon as Mr. Wilson began talking, I understood Lorrel's admiration and love. I was intrigued to learn that Lorrel was not Mr. Wilson's grandson by birth, but by marriage. The younger man's words of admiration and affection gave no indication of an "in-law" relationship.

Sharing his story was important to Mr. Wilson. He wanted to pass on the lessons of his life to his family. Early in the process, he augmented his words by showing me photos, paintings, and even drawing the floor plan of his childhood home. He would patiently repeat stories to make sure I had heard and transcribed his words as he wanted. If he wasn't sure that his words were clear enough, particularly about an action, he would stand and try to demon-strate for me. He did this so often that I stopped putting the mike on his shirt and just left it on the table. Mr. Wilson tried to answer every question I posed. When he became impatient with himself for not remembering a detail quickly enough, he would tap his fingers on the table until the memory returned. If he was still unable to remember, he whistled for Willie Mae to come and help.

Willie Mae, who is called Tillie by her family, is a petite woman. Like her father, she has a ready smile and radiates warmth. As our meetings continued, Willie Mae often joined us, sometimes listening, sometimes providing details or asking questions, always prompting more memories. Over time, Willie Mae began adding stories and details of her own.

After my initial trepidation, I always looked forward to being with Mr. Wilson. At the beginning of our relationship, I was simply the means to an end. Mr. Wilson wanted to tell his story and I was there to help him. Later we grew to enjoy being together, our conversation moving beyond his memories to whatever was happening in the world. Often when he joined me in the kitchen, he approached with a sprightly pace, and a big smile on his face saying, "Hello Susie." He was the only person outside of my older relatives who called me Susie. I continued to call him Mr. Wilson.

Mr. Wilson and I worked together for almost two years, generally meeting several times a month, with our schedule broken only by travels. During the first visit, Mr. Wilson outlined his life. Then, as we continued to work together, we slowly filled in the details. Throughout, Mr. Wilson continued to be enthusiastic and thoughtful about telling his story with as much detail as possible. Although we talked of his adult life, for him, the core of both his being and his story were in Bunkie and Meeker, the Louisiana towns where he had grown to adulthood. He began with, and kept returning to, the time in his life that for him was most pivotal—the early deaths of his parents, particularly his father. Johnnie Wilson Sr. played a key role in his son's identity, and his death haunted Mr. Wilson throughout his life.

Johnnie Wilson's story is, as much as possible, in his own words. I transcribed his syntax and words as he spoke them, making changes only as necessary to connect and clarify the story. Following Mr. Wilson's death, I added details of stories learned from Willie Mae, Betty, Lorrel, and Mr. Wilson's brother, George. Only those details known by Mr. Wilson were used.

Johnnie Wlson survived difficult circumstances through strength of character he attributed to his father. He passed his lessons and warmth on to his family and to those who knew him. From him I have learned about generosity of spirit, forgiveness, acceptance and tenacity. Each time I was with him, I left with far more than when I had arrived and I continue to view and react to the world with a different vision because of him.

The story begins where Mr. Wilson began telling it, in his raspy, almost whispery voice.

Tone in the Bell

WHAT I WANT TO TALK ABOUT IS THAT I LOST MY MOTHER AND FATHER. They died. They got poisoned. My family started to fall apart when I was eleven years old and I lost my father, mother, oldest brother and two sisters.

Everything was fine until we moved away from a house where we was living to a new place when I was seven years old. The new house was closer to Cheneyville than Bunkie, but our town was still Bunkie. Bunkie's a real small town south of Alexandria in central Louisiana. There was a bank and maybe four or five stores. The bank was at one end of town and the train station was over aways. All around Cheneyville and Bunkie was farmland and bayous. Bayous are like little rivers. They make the land good for farming.

This new farm was not the first farm my Daddy owned. I don't know how he got the first one, but I know for sure he bought this last one. I know because I used to go in his buggy with him when he went to see Johnny Rhodes, the man in the bank that he bought the farm from.

I remember Johnny Rhodes so good because my mother ironed shirts for him. The banker lived right close to the bank. Me and my oldest brother, Curly, used to go to town in the buggy with my mother and carry the shirts to him after my mother ironed them. We carried the shirts to his house all the time. Nice big house by itself. We just open the door and put the shirts in. The door stayed open all the time. Mr. Rhodes musta had no wife cause I never did see no woman there. He had no wife or we'd a saw her sometime. The house wouldn't have been open like that if she'd a been there.

I don't know if Mr. Rhodes owned the bank or what. I only know he worked there. He had to have some position at the bank to be doing what he was doing to help Daddy. I don't know why he helped Daddy, maybe because Daddy knew how to treat people. He learned me how to treat people. That's how I learned how to do everything, from my daddy. I ain't nothing but a kid when I went with my daddy to the bank, but listening to them talk, I'm learning from what they say and how they say it. As I grow up, it stays with me, know how to treat people, how to handle 'em. From that day to this day, I'm the same way. I get along with everybody.

The new farm my daddy bought was big enough to have three houses for the people working for him and a big family house for us. The houses were made of wood and had shingled roofs. Our house was on one side of the lot, and the other three on the other side. From our house to the others was about three blocks long. On the other side of the lot gate was woods. There was a bridge that went across the Bayou Boeuf *(pronounced "Bar Bef" by Mr. Wilson)* but we didn't have to go to the bayou to bring water to the house to drink or take a bath no more. No, no. A big cistern furnished all the water we needed in our house for drinking and bathing. That cistern sure made life easier.

When my daddy bought the farm, the white man who lived there did not want to leave the big house. He didn't want no black man moving into his house. He liked to kill Daddy. We had a lot of trouble getting him out of the house. For almost a year after Daddy bought the farm we lived in one of the smaller farm houses until the white man moved. I don't know how Daddy finally got the man to move, but he did. Even after that man moved, he stayed nearby, right around Bayou Boeuf, on the other side of the bayou, right in front of the house where we were living. We on this side of the bayou, he on the other.

Our house was a nice fine house, with big trees in the yard that gave lots of shade in the summer. Some were fig trees, but I don't think there were other fruit trees there then. Later on I planted peach trees with Daddy. Our house was so nice with a porch that ran all around it. I loved it so to get up early and walk all around and look at the trees. Every morning I would get up and walk all the way around the house.

We had five rooms without the kitchen. The kitchen was big enough to put a bedroom in there if we needed to. Just that big. My parents had one bedroom. My brothers and I shared another room and my sisters had a private room with their own door going outside. Two of the bedrooms had armoires where we kept our clothes.

I remember the armoires real good because one day I was standing near the one in my parents' room with Curly. Somehow he got hold of Daddy's razor and cut my arm; deep cut. He didn't know what he was doing, just doing something. Mama put a spider web on it to heal it. I still got a scar from that cut, but it healed just fine.[i]

There was a gate about twenty feet in front of the house. Outside the fence that ran all around the house was another fenced-in yard where the chickens and hogs were kept. On the other side of the gate of the chicken and hog pen was a bridge. You had to cross the bridge to go on the road. The road turn just like Bayou Boeuf do. You go to the left, follow the road right on around, you go to Cheneyville. You go to the right, you go to Bunkie.

My daddy, he'd open that gate for the four mules to go out, and they'd walk to that bridge and drink. When the mules finished drinking, they'd walk back up to the lot that was far from the house, about the same as three city blocks away. Next to that was the lot where Daddy grew the corn and everything. A lot of time when Daddy closed the gate, his best friend, George Johnson, crossed the bridge and talk to him. They would talk all the time. George Johnson lived right at the other end of the bridge, near where that white man live.

My daddy, Johnny—I got his name—was about six feet tall. I'm just the same height as he was. He weighed about two hundred pounds. My mother, Siphronia Sibley Wilson, was a small woman, only about five feet, three or four inches. She only weighed about 145 lbs. My mother took care of the house, the cooking and worked in the fields with the rest of us.

Daddy was a big farmer. He had six people working for him and he made a good farm every year. They raised everything they needed on the farm. Daddy raised sugar cane and made his own syrup. Sugar cane grows as high as ten to twelve feet. You take it and put it down and cut the top off. This little cane you see here in the stores, that ain't nothin but trash. He also raised cotton, corn, sweet potatoes and popcorn. We had plenty of everything— chickens, hogs, guineas, and ducks. You name it, we had them. We ate real good. My father was a good farmer and knew how to take care of business. He was doing fine there and we all had plenty of everything. Even had a wagon and a buggy. Never had to borrow nothing from nobody.

Daddy and Mama got along just like two peas in one hole. That's the way they got along. I never known my Mama or my Daddy ever cross a word. Never heard them squabble or spat. No bad language between them. No, no. That's why you never hear me say bad language. Never. Between me and my wife, she never heard me say a bad word to her. Willie Mae has never heard me say a bad word or cuss. Never. How angry I get, I never get angry enough to use bad language. No, no, cause I wasn't raised like that. I never had no problems with nobody coming up because I got my style from them. I was never fighting, or getting into things cause that's the way they lived and that's the way I live. That's why everybody likes me, cause I never bother nobody.

There was seven of us children living at home. My oldest brother, Curly, was born in 1901. Then came my sister Maggie. I was the third child, born on June 19, 1903. After me came Coleman, George, Alice and Henry. George, Alice and Henry were born after we moved to the farm. No, no. I just say Alice. I remember all of their names but hers. I can't think of her name, so I just give her that name.[ii] I don't remember Mommy or Daddy ever punishing us. You never hear my parents holler or fuss at us. I don't know, there just never was no squabbling amongst the kids or nothing like that. Curly fight, but not with us. We just get along.

After we moved to the new farm, I started working out in the fields with my daddy, just to be with him. I learned how to plow and help him in the fields. I was the only one that went everywhere he go. Everywhere he went, I was right there with him, doing anything he needed that I could do. I just wanted to help him. My daddy was always working and talking to himself, laughing, planning. He was jolly; all the time jolly. I liked being with him and learning how he do things. I just wanted to be a man like my daddy.

One morning after we were in the house for a couple of years, I got up to take my walk around the house. I saw a piece of paper just outside the first gate. I walked to the gate, opened it, picked that paper up and I looked at it. It had a picture of a baby cradle drawn on the paper with some writing on there. I carried it back into Mama. She looked at it and read the words out loud, "from the cradle on up." That's what it said on there. I didn't know what it meant then. Later I figure the note was a warning.

In a year's time, after we got the note, Alice died. She was about two years old, just as cute as she could be. I never knowed anyone say what's wrong with her. Nobody else took sick then. A year later when I was eleven, my daddy, my mama, Curly and Maggie all took sick. Daddy got so sick that he couldn't work no more, just laying there in the bed sick. My brother and my sister, too. All sick in the bed. None of them could get out of bed. My mother was still able to get around. I don't remember how they was sick, if they was in pain or what, I only know they was just too sick to get out of bed.

The people who worked for my father kept working for him, so we still had food. One day in April or May I could see them going through the yard to get to the fields to chop the cotton. At that time, I was the only one that was big enough and healthy enough to sit and fan my father while he lay in the bed.

My father lay there, facing the window. My mother came through the bedroom, looked at him and went through the door that led from the bedroom to the porch. She sat down on a chair on the porch. I could see her through the window that was at the foot of Daddy's bed, sitting on the porch, looking away from the house to the yard and the front gate. As Daddy lay there, his knee was bent up. When he start to die, his knee straighten out. His knee got right down, and he close his eyes, and he just pass away.

He died about one o'clock in the afternoon. I could see my mother sitting on the porch start to cry. She wasn't looking in the window. She didn't see my daddy die, but she start to cry just as soon as he start to die. I never could figure out how she knew at just that moment that he died.

About twenty minutes later Maggie, who was lying in the other room, wanted to see my father. Even though she was older than me, her head only came up to the top of my shoulder. I brought Maggie in to see him. She stood at the bed and looked at him for a few minutes. Then I carried her back to bed, and just twenty minutes later she was dead too.

When Maggie died, I just went off. I was just out of my mind. I didn't know nothing until I was standing there and I come to. I didn't know what to think. I was just looking; out of my mind. I just stand there, looking. Finally I got straightened out and knew what they were doing. They's burying them in the ground. They was putting dirt on them. Where I was all that time between when they died and when they were buried, or what I did, I don't know. I knowed nothing 'til they was putting them in the ground. I don't know whether I was dead or alive. I don't know. It was a mystery, a mystery.

My father and sister were buried right side to side at a big church in Eola about two miles from home. When he was alive my daddy was not a church going man. He'd go to church sometime with my mother and us kids, but not every Sunday like she did. Daddy got his religion on his deathbed. They come there to sprinkle him and baptize him. He got sprinkled by another church, not my mother's.

The church where my father and sister were buried had a bell way up in a steeple. When somebody die, they rang what's called "tone in the bell." They rang the bell one time and stopped. Then they'd pull it again and stop. That's letting you know somebody's dead. You could hear the bell from our house two miles away, just like it was across the street. The sound of that bell come right down the water and you could hear plain; you know somebody's dead when they tone that bell. Later on a storm took that bell right out of the steeple and set it on the ground.

It was hard after my daddy died. All of the farm workers moved out right away. When Daddy and Maggie died, Mama was left with five sons. Curly, the oldest was sick already, but the rest of us, including Henry who was only six months old were okay. My mother moved us all out of the big house. We had figured out that someone had put poison in the cistern and she wanted to get us away. I never got sick because I never drank much water. We moved into one of the houses where the workers had lived. After we moved out of the big house, no one lived there. If she don't move out that house, all of us, Coleman, George, Henry and I would have been dead too. My daddy's sister Adeline, who we called Aunt Nan, come and take Henry with her. Mama was sick and she couldn't take care of him no more.

Before my father got sick and died, he was a very independent man, a strong man. He was a big farmer. He made a good farm every year. Lots of people didn't like him because he was a big farmer and independent. I think that the white guy who had to move out of the big house for my father was the one who poisoned my family. The white guy and George Johnson, my daddy's best friend, were both jealous of my daddy's success. The white man hated Daddy and could have shot him down with a gun, hated him just that bad. They figured some way to do it besides shooting him. They got together and put something in that cistern, some kind of poison or something. We always thought that George was the one who put the poison in the cistern for the white man. We don't got no proof, but it had to be him and the white man that did it, cause there was no-body else around but them two. That's why they say, "You better watch your best friend when they think you got more than they got." It just destroyed my family.

There weren't many black men who owned farms where we were. Most worked for white men. Black men owning farms in Louisiana didn't have long lives. They didn't want us to have nothing. It was just lucky if they don't do something. If you got your own farm and were independent, and don't have to go to them for nothing, they don't like that. No, no. They don't like that. They could do whatever they wanted to. They know nothing gonna be done about it. It was just so pitiful.

I know of another man that got killed too. About a mile and a half from where I lived later with my grandfather, near a town called Cheneyville, a black man named Shelly Wade lived. Mr. Wade owned his own farm just like my daddy. He had two sons and one daughter, I think. When I was about seventeen, they wrote him a "black hand" letter telling him to bring so much money to Lecompte right where the train take water. There was a big water tank there. Next to the water tank on the side of the highway was a big 3-1/2 foot high cement block. The note told him to put that money there, right on that block.

Shelly's son brought him there. When Shelly put the money on the block, they shot him. His son liked to got killed too, but they wasn't after the son. They was only after Shelly. That's just what happened to him. They killed him right there on the spot. That was so pitiful. I still remember it just like it happened yesterday. I remember it. His death just live with me. I would wake up at five o'clock in the morning sometimes and think about it. It's just something that lives with me. It's just a hurting thing to me when they do a family like that for no reason.

I don't know how we survived. We just survived some kind of way. We had a garden, and had plenty of syrup, enough to last a couple of years, because Daddy had raised a lot of sugar cane. We had syrup on everything. And we caught fish.

My mother died almost a year later, in March, 1916. When she was sick, Uncle Cliff take her to Bunkie to catch the train to go to Alexandria to the doctor. We stayed by ourselves. Her family checked up on us. My older brother Curly was with us, but he was sick and I looked after my brothers. I was twelve years old.

Mama was away for about a week. They couldn't do her no good. My aunt and uncle say she had ulcers. They brought her right back to that house. There was nobody to see after her. She passed away about three days after they brought her back. Mama was buried at the cemetery of the church she belonged to in Bunkie. The church sat on a high hill near farms. The graveyard not far from the church.

We had very little food after my mother died. All we really had to eat was syrup. That's all we had. I hid it under the house so my Uncle Cliff couldn't find it. If he find it, he take it and sell it. He had a house full of children. You don't know what people will do when they're hungry. I had to hide the syrup. It was all we had to eat.

There was nobody to run the farm after Daddy and Mama died. The farm probably went back to the bank.

All Scattered Around

AFTER MAMA DIED, WE WAS ALL SCATTERED AROUND. GEORGE, WHO WAS about six, went to my mother's brother, Harrison Sibley, and his family in Beaumont, Texas. My uncle died a few years later, and my aunt Elise moved to Los Angeles with her two children. Elise told her son, Charles, that George didn't want to move to Los Angeles with them and that his Aunt Nan was taking George from her. It wasn't that George didn't want to move with them. Elise didn't want to take the responsibility for raising George, who was her husband's nephew. Charles hated that so bad, hated it that George wasn't going with them. But he never knowed no different. After we got grown, I wouldn't tell him. Just make him feel bad. George went to live with Nan who was already raising Henry. She finished raising George.

Coleman went to live with my Daddy's brother, Coleman, in Houston. My oldest brother, Curly, and I went to live with my granddaddy, Phillip Wilson, in Meeker, about five miles north of Bunkie. Grandpa and Grandma come get Curly and me in a wagon. Curly, who was sick when my mother was alive, lasted until we were at my grandfather's for about eight months. When he passed, we had to carry him in a wagon to bury him where my mother was buried in Bunkie. Once I was at Grandpa's, I didn't see my other brothers much 'til we got grown.

I never saw my grandfather or grandmother before I went to live with them on the farm where they lived. Something must have happened between my father and Grandpa too, because my father never saw him. We never went to see him, and he never come to see us. That shows how far they was apart, cause we didn't live that far away, only five miles or so.

They lived on a big place near the woods. Couldn't get to the house unless you go through the woods. Don't know why I didn't get snake bit and get killed. Out all hours of the night, walking through the woods. Never saw a snake. Not one time. I know they was there though.

I don't know if Grandpa was renting the farm or what.[iii] It was such a big place, one person couldn't work all the land. It was too big. He raised sugar cane and corn. He also raised hogs. My granddaddy always raised hogs. He'd kill the hogs in the winter and smoke them in his smoke house. His smoke house was about six feet by ten feet. It had pieces of wood that ran all the way across the ceiling to hang the meat on to smoke. That meat was smoked just like you get smoked meat here, now. He smoked that meat real good. Grandpa also made his own sausage. He'd take them cuts off the hog and make that sausage, put that spout on the sausage grinder and grind that meat. I remember watching him grind the meat and stuff the casings. He'd take them sausages and put them on the rack and smoke them. Now, you're talking about something real good.

Uncle Cliff, one of my father's brothers, and his family lived about two miles away from Grandpa, and Uncle Phillip, the youngest brother and his wife and three kids lived in another house at the same place as Grandpa. Before I come to my grandfather's, Uncle Phillip worked at a sawmill and got hurt there. He didn't have his right mind because of the hurt. I don't know what happened to him, got hit in the head or something. Phillip was all right if everything went along all right. But Grandpa, he'd fuss at him. That would make Phillip upset. He don't know what he's doing hardly. If it was calm, he had no problem. When he was calm, he was just like anybody else. You would think nothing was wrong.

Well, my grandfather squabbled with Phillip all the time. Grandpa was so mean to Phillip that Phillip just left him when I was about fifteen. He moved to a great big farm through the woods, the same as about two blocks away. When he left Grandpa, Phillip didn't have no more problems. He took good care of his family.

I was the only one to do the work after Phillip left. Sometimes my grandfather would hire someone to help pick the cotton. There was one guy, for one or two years, come there and work some of that land. But he left, and there was nobody but me. I had to do all the plowing myself. I pulled the corn too. I was a big boy working in the field doing all the work. Grandpa couldn't work cause he was too old. In the summer when school was out, Nan's son, Willie Synoque, would come and help me. Henry and George never came in the summer. They stayed and worked at Nan's place. She kept them working.

Grandpa couldn't do nothing but fuss. He whoop me for nothing. That's all he could do. Grandma, she couldn't work. She just do the cooking. As mean as my grandfather was to me, he was never mean to my grandmother, Luticia. He was nice to Grandma cause she'd fuss at him, not much, just to let him know that he couldn't run over her. So that would cool him off. They got along just fine, but he treated me like I was a dog or something. He didn't have nobody to do nothing for him but me. How could he be like that? I never understood why Grandpa was so mean to me since he needed me to do the work. I did all the work, everything. He just sat on the porch as mean as anything you could ever see.

Sometimes on Saturdays, if I did all my work, cut wood, everything, my grandfather give me a quarter and let me go to the store. I had to be back there when it was 3:00. He knew it was 3:00 because the train going to Alexandria would pass and blow its whistle. He'd be sitting on the porch waiting with the buggy whip across his lap. If I wasn't at the gate at 3:00, if it was just five minutes after that train passed, he get off the porch, meet me halfway between the porch and gate and beat me with that buggy whip. I just stand there, let him whoop me. Miserable life. I'd go on the back porch, sit down and cry. I still have marks on my back now where he whoop me with that buggy whip.

It was tough. Couldn't be no worse than that. But I growed up just like my daddy started me. No matter what Grandpa did, I just went along with it. As bad as he treat me, I went along with it, stayed with him. I can't run off. I don't know where to go.

My grandfather's meanness never stopped. My grandma, she never took up for me. She never told him, "You ain't got nobody to help you. Why you doing him like that?" She told me that if I run off, the cops would get me. That's what she told me. He treat me so bad, and that's all she'd say. She wouldn't try to stop him or nothing. That's the hurting part, that she never said, "You shouldn't do him like that. You ain't got nobody to work and help you." That's just the way they was. I think she might have been afraid to stand up to him about me, but it still hurt. He must have been raised up awful bad for him to be mean to me like he was. Now, that's me saying that with all that he did to me. Got to be something the cause of it.

It's interesting. My daddy and his brothers were nice, but my Grandpa and Auntie Nan were terrible. She was evil. Nan wasn't so bad with me cause I didn't see her much til I was already a young man. She couldn't do nothing to me. Nan wasn't that mean to Henry, but George was the one that had the bad time with her. I finally had to take George away from her because she treated him so bad. She was just so mean. Her son Willie was a year older than me. She sent him off to school every year, but wouldn't let George or Henry go. They had to work.

I don't know much about my grandfather. He never talked about much. He was so mean and hateful, I never thought to ask him about his life. I never thought one time to ask him did he have any brothers or sisters. Never asked him cause I was scared of him. If I coulda talked to him, asked him about his people or something, then I would know something about them. He had to have been a slave, but I don't know for a fact. I don't know anything. I don't know his date of birth or anything.

This white guy lived in the woods below us. He always came right through the yard, past the porch with his mules, all the time. He come that way cause it's closer to go to town. Sometimes he'd stop and talk to Grandpa. One day a couple of years after I was there, he come through there like he always did. Grandpa was sitting on the porch with a gun across his lap. When the man got close to the house, Grandpa stood up, made the man back his mules up and go around the longer way through the gate. Why he would do something like that I would just like to know. What reason would he have to do that? I couldn't ask him cause he could have killed me; he's just that mean. The man had passed through there all the time. The man didn't do him nothing. After so long of letting the man take the shorter way, I would like to know why on that day he made him go back. They could have come there one o'clock in the morning, set the house on fire and burn all of us up. I don't know why they didn't. They coulda. No one woulda done nothing.

That's just something to think about.

My Uncle Coleman would sometimes send Grandpa a package from Houston and I'd go to the post office to get it. I was a big boy then, thirteen, something like that. But I couldn't sign my name because I ain't never been to school. My Daddy and Mommy got along so well on the farm they just forgot to send us to school, so I never went. I signed with an "X."

One time a white man standing there said, "Look at him. As big as he is he can't sign his own name." He kept looking at me as I walked out of the post office. It hurt me so bad I went to crying once I got outside.

My grandfather thought about sending me to school when I first went to live with him. He even got me new clothes. I think he sent all of his children. I know my Uncle Phillip had a good education. He had as pretty a handwriting as you could ever see.

But one day these two old people, fortunetellers or something, come back there in the woods and told Grandpa, "Don't send him to school. If you send him to school, he'll go crazy." So Grandpa, he didn't send me.

On the side of the road near where I lived was an old abandoned Caterpillar machine. I would go by the machine a lot. I knew the name of the machine. Every time I would go by the machine I would spell that name, "caterpillar" and learned the letters. I could spell "caterpillar" before I could spell "rat" or "cat." I started to write with a stick on the ground, just marking on the ground. That's how I got started learning to read and write.

I figured out words anyway I could. Once I saw a boy, about eight or nine years old, in front of a store window with a sign in it. I asked him, "Do you know what that is?"

He said, "Soda water." He knew how to read the words, but I didn't. Now, he didn't know that I didn't know what it was. And so I learned two new words. That's just how I kept learning. Every way I could, I figured out new words. Every little thing I see, I tried to write. I just kept on and taught myself to read and write. I don't have education, but I can read and write. Later I learned to write better by watching my Uncle Phillip.

One day when I must have been about sixteen, a young man came to my Granddaddy's and said he was my brother. So he was my brother I guess. I never saw him 'til then.

I don't know how he found his way back there from where he lived, but he did. His name was James, but we called him "Monk." I don't know why, but that's what we called him. He was about one year older than me and had lived with his mother 'til then. Monk stayed close by and lived on a nearby farm. He became like another brother to me. Besides Monk, I didn't see my other brothers for a long time. Coleman was in Texas, too far to see, and Henry and George were with my Aunt Nan.

After a few years, my brother Coleman came to live with me at my grandfather's. He came to live with us cause they couldn't do nothing with him. He was devilish. Uncle Coleman was never home—playing pool and stuff and his wife couldn't do nothing with Coleman. When he come out of school, he just do as he want to do, you know. He was raised up in the country, and he used to certain ways. After school, he go by the store. They set the bananas out and apples out. He see them and just go in there and get him one. Finally they watched him and told them if it happened again, they was gonna have to do something about it. They had to send him to Grandpa.

When Coleman came to live with us, he gave me my second nickname. When I was little, at home with Daddy and Mama, they called me T.T. I don't remember why. None of my other brothers or sisters had nicknames then. Later on we called George "Cap" cause he always wore a hat. No one around my grandfather's house called me T.T. I left that name back home. At Grandpa's, since I was a real good checker player, they started calling me "Checker Papa." That name stuck for a long time. From that they went to calling me "Pop." Now, everybody calls me "Pop."

My grandfather did Coleman the same as me. The only difference is that Coleman ran off and left. I didn't. I was afraid to leave until I was eighteen. At first, Coleman didn't go too far, just to a big farm, owned by the Bowmans, that was about the same as three blocks away, just through the woods. The farm had a row of houses for all the people living there. There were about thirty-five head of mule used to work that farm, that's how big it was. He didn't stay there long. He went on to Galveston, Texas with a man named Clarence Reed. He went to Texas when he was sixteen.

For awhile when I was seventeen and still living with my grandparents, I worked at Emil Jurett's farm. His farm was real close to where Grandpa and Grandma lived. They raised cotton and sugar cane. People came from a lot of different places to work on that farm. I earned extra money and could buy Grandma some coffee and sugar, you know. I worked at that farm until I got eighteen, until I was a man.

My grandpa was still misusing me, so when I turned eighteen, I just run off and left them. If they be nice to me, I'd stay, cause they had nobody else to help em. They couldn't do it theirself. After I moved away I wanted to go back and take them something, but I was scared. Mean as he was he like to get that shotgun and kill me before I got to the house. I was just that scared of him.

I don't know who helped my grandparents out after I left. I don't know if Phillip or Cliff did, cause he treated them so bad too. I didn't see my grandparents again until I was thirty-five years old. Over the years I thought about visiting them, but I was afraid that my grandfather would shoot me for running off. My Daddy's sister, Nan, take me to see them. I brought Willie Mae with me. That's the only time she saw them and the last time I saw them. By the time I saw them, they had moved to another place in Lecompte.

My grandfather was sitting there fishing on the bayou when I got there. He had a long buffalo fish that he had caught laying by his side. I walked up to him and shook his hand. He knew me. All them years, he knew me. We talked a little. He looked just like he did when I first saw him with his long white beard. He had to be over a hundred when he died. Grandma was still alive then too, but she was in the bed, sick. She was happy to see us.

That Was Some Kind of Time

WHEN I FIRST RUN OFF, I WENT TO WORK AT THE RAILROAD ON AN EXTRA gang. We lived right on the railroad tracks. They give us cars to live in. Our job was to take railroad ties out or put them back in the tracks. I worked there about a month when the gang moved. I was scared to go with them cause I didn't want to go that far away from Meeker. I ain't never been nowhere else and I was scared to follow. I went to the railroad at Lecompte near my Aunt Nan's and was hired. I worked there about three weeks. They found out I wasn't twenty-one, so they fired me.

After that I went to work on the Canebreak Farm, owned by the Bowmans, back near my grandfather's. It was a big farm—at least two and a half miles around. They raised sugar cane, plenty corn and plenty of cotton. They raised so much cotton that they could carry three bales of cotton to the gin at the same time. A big wagon hold three bales, way up there. Used to pick it and weigh it and throw it in the wagon right there, 'til they get about three bales, then add to another wagon that was right there waiting. At the cotton gin, they'd suck out a bale of cotton at a time—suck out a bale the first time, next time half of what's left. Each bale weighed about four, five hundred pounds.

A lot of people come from different places to work at Canebreak Farm. There had to be around fifty-five or sixty people who lived and worked on the farm. When I first went there, I asked my Uncle Phillip could I stay with him. He told me, "Yeah." That's where I started from there.

Other people came in from town to work each day. A big wagon go to town and bring people back there just to work and then bring them back to town in the evening. That was nice of them to run the wagon. The foreman had a big bell at his house that he would ring in the morning to get people up to go to work. You could hear that bell way out. We even heard it at my grandfather's house some miles away.

The Bowmans who owned the farm were nice people to work for. The bossman's son, Edward, loved me. When I moved to the farm, Edward must have been about ten years old. He liked me because I never was a guy always fussing, and I'd take up time with him. Me and him go places in the fields. He was always around with me. It was quite natural I'd like him. He was a nice young man, a nice young man.

Edward Bowman told a young woman, Clara Reed, about me. Edward wanted Clara to like me and told her, "Clara, that's a fine boy." She was the sister of the man Coleman went to Galveston with. Clara's family lived on the Bowman farm. Her parents, Lutishie and George, had a lot of kids working for this place and the Bowmans built them their own house. Lutishie just stayed there and didn't work nowhere but her own house, taking care of her kids. Lutishie was joyful with everyone and everyone loved her. All of her grown children would come together in the winter and kill the hogs and do all the boiling and smoking. You do the hogs during the winter when it was cold so it would keep. They smoked it to preserve it for the summer.

Clara was the eighth in her family. There were ten. She was only 4 foot ten inches. Clara was so short, she was too short to work in the field, so she worked in the house with the bossman's wife. Working in the house made it just nice for her.

But when he pointed me out, Clara told her sister, "I don't like that old long-legged boy." That was fine with me cause I was young and wasn't thinking about no marriage.

Nothing happened with Clara until her sister, Margaret, who everyone called Bluchie said, "Well, I like him. You tell him so for me. I like him." When Bluchie said this, Clara switched around. I know she said to herself, "Well, if Bluchie like him, she must see something good about him." So Clara got to liking me herself. I liked Clara almost from the beginning because she's nice and quiet. She never talked that much. Even when she get angry she stay quiet.

Me and her kept going together. Time passed by and we got married on July 20, 1925. I was twenty-two. We got married at her mother's house. Lutishie cooked real good; a whole lot of food. There were so many people, you couldn't keep in the house. All around the house is trees and people was up in trees looking down. So many people was there cause I was well known. A lot of people know me by my playing ball.

Clara and I had a good life together. We always got along just fine. I never had problems after we were married. I never was the kind to squabble, but if we did, I'd find somewhere to stay for two or three hours. When I got back, everything was okay. Later when I had a truck, I'd take a long drive, then come back later. To just stay there and holler, day in and day out, you'd drive your own self crazy. We never had no arguments that we gonna worry about and dislike each other. No, nothing like that.

Our first child was born exactly one year to the day after we got married. We named her Bertha Mae. We were so crazy about the baby. Bertha Mae slept in our bed, in the middle of Clara and me. One night soon after she was born, I woke up and saw Bertha Mae was dead. She had been bleeding through her nose. Somehow Clara must have hit Bertha Mae in the head with her elbow. Oh, that was a hurting thing. That was a hurting thing. It shouldn't happen like that.

Our second daughter, Willie Mae, was born one year after Bertha Mae on June 14, 1927. We had a third daughter, Lillie Mae, born in 1928. When she was about two and a half years old, she died of thrush. Willie Mae is the only one of her generation. My brothers, Coleman and George, never had children. I'm the only one who had any. Coleman's wife had one sister and two brothers—didn't none of them have any children either. That's kind of peculiar.

When Willie Mae was little, I carried her everywhere I went. Everywhere I went walking, she'd always go with me. I don't know where Clara at. Just me and Willie Mae. Yeah. When Willie Mae do go with Clara, Clara walk fast and Willie Mae had to run to keep up. Clara always do that. I always fussed at Clara about making Willie Mae run. I fuss at her, "Don't make her run like that! Walk slow."

Clara's sister, Bluchie, lived about five miles from where we were. Sometimes Clara and Willie Mae get up early in the morning, before the sun came up, and walk down to Bluchie's. They stay the day and come back. Bluchie didn't have no children and she was very clean and strict. Willie Mae had to be careful not to touch things. After awhile Bluchie started getting pregnant and had one kid after the other. Then she wasn't so strict.

As soon as I was able and could get a place with enough room, my brothers came to live with us. George was the first. I brought him from Aunt Nan's cause it wasn't good for him to stay there. She living near us now after she moved back from her other place. She so mean. George don't being doing nothing; she haul off and hit him. I knew she was evil, but I didn't know some until George told me.

He told me that when he was about 13, he worked on the farm near the machine that picked the cane up and took it up to the wagon. Another boy and him walked behind the machine and picked up cane the machine missed. The rope broke and they couldn't trip the cane right. The man called him up to take the rope. He doing that and then the fly wheel caught his foot and rubbed it until they could stop it. They took him to the hospital. He was there two or three weeks. He went back to Nan's house. He had to crawl through the house, crawl where he wanted to go. Nan come in and say, "How come you didn't do such and such a thing. Then she catch him upside the head. Why she do that to him? He can't do nothing but crawl. He had no crutch or nothing until he find an old broom in her kitchen and used it for a crutch. Then he could get around better.

One day when Willie Mae was still a baby, I was visiting George and Henry at Nan's. At that time, she was next door to me at the farm. She had separated from her husband. George came in after working and saw a piece of sausage on the stove. He was hungry so he ate the sausage. Nan was so angry he ate it, she got some scissors and was going to stab him. Just cause he ate some sausage. I grabbed her and take the scissors from her. George got a chair turned over backwards and was gonna knock her in the head with the chair.

I said, "Come on, let's go. I'm gonna take you with me." If I didn't take him to stay with me, I know something's gonna happen. She just that mean. Later, George lived and worked with me at the sawmill. Then Henry come to live with us. By then, George and his wife, Edna, lived at the same place, but in his own house and Henry lived with me and Clara. Whenever we could, we lived together and helped take care of each other. I wanted my family together.

When we were grown, Henry was the smallest out of all of us, but still he was bigger than Monk. I was the tallest, but George and Coleman were both big men. George is larger than I am, maybe. He's not as tall, but he is bigger. He and Coleman each weighed about 200 pounds.

I always tried to keep the peace and gave in to them a lot. I was always the calm one of the brothers. I never raised no sand. The hardest one to keep peace with was Coleman. Coleman was the one of us, after Curly, who raised all the sand. He was always getting angry about something. He was a nice guy, a nice guy, but he sure did love to drink and fuss. The rest of my brothers were more like me. George, he's kind of quiet, too. He never raised no sand. Henry didn't raise no sand. No. And, Monk neither.

George and I bought a Chevrolet together. We saw this car. George had thirty dollars. I had about the same. We decided to get this car. So we did. Only trouble with that was neither one of us could drive. The man who sold us the car wanted to help us out. He's gonna teach us to drive. George told me to do it. I did. The man carried us around and show us how to shift the car.

Then the man said, "Go down this road here. You don't meet many cars down this road." That's the way we went home. I did the shift and George steered the car. When we got home, we drove up in the yard. There was a big old canal at the side of the house. I told George, "Be sure to keep your foot on the brakes." He did. We finally stopped in time. Later, George kept backing up and trying, backing up and trying til he learnt how to shift.

We loved that car. One time me and George were going off. I didn't know that Clara wanted to come with us. She got on the back fender holding Willie Mae. We started the car, and they fell off into the sawdust. Glad we wasn't going fast.

While I was in the fields, Clara took care of the bossman's children. She put them all around the stove when she cooked. Sometimes she would take Willie Mae along with her when she took care of them. Most of the time when Clara worked, her younger sister, Nora, would keep Willie Mae during the day. One time when Nora keep Willie Mae, Willie Mae got an empty syrup bucket on her head and it wouldn't come off. Nora tried to pull the bucket off Willie Mae's head, but it got caught on her ears. She couldn't move that bucket. Just couldn't get that ole bucket off. She didn't know what to do so she come get Clara and me from work. I cut the bucket off Willie Mae's head. Willie Mae was scared and sticky from the syrup. She never did that again. Makes me laugh now remembering.

Every day at twelve o'clock I'd lay down the plow and ride a mule home for dinner. I'd have lunch with Willie Mae and Clara. After lunch when it was time to go back to the fields, Willie Mae be sitting on the porch. We had nice quarters. There was a porch on the quarters that was real wide. When I go back to the fields, I had to lean way over on the mule so she couldn't see my head, cause she see my head, she gonna cry. She'd go to crying if I straighten up so she could see me. She didn't want me to go back to work.

I first learned how to play baseball when I was young and still living at my granddaddy's. Every day at twelve o'clock the men on the Bowman farm would play ball and I'd go over there and play with them out in the big pasture. Sometimes it was so hot you'd be wringing wet, but when it's something you like, you just do it. When the bell rang they all go back to work, wringing wet, didn't make no difference. Yeah, and I go back across the woods to my grandfather's.

One of the things I wanted to do was learn a trick with the ball. Back then a lot of players did tricks. I wanted to have the ball between my heels and jump up to throw the ball up with my heels so that the ball came up over my head where I could catch it. I had a hard time learning it. I tried almost a year. I was almost about to give up. But one day, I went out there, put the ball between my heels, kicked the ball up. Just as I throw it up I looked around at the same time. The ball come right over, right by my head, just where I want it to go. I just kept doing that 'til I got it perfect.

I learned to pitch by looking at different guys pitch, see how they throw and see how they catch it. That's how I learned to do it. There was a chimney on the east side of my grandfather's house. I'd throw the ball against the chimney, practicing my pitching. I became a good pitcher. I could throw a ball straight at someone, and that ball would break away from the person at the last minute without hitting him.

After I was married I started playing on the Meeker Dirty Devils baseball team. We only played on the weekends because we all had to work during the week. George, Henry and Monk played on the same baseball team as me. Henry played first base or outfield, George outfield and catcher, Monk was the catcher and I was the pitcher. Coleman was in Galveston and never did play with us. He's the only one who didn't.

Tom Porter was our team manager. He knows just how to handle men, to get more out of them. No fussing and hollering at 'em. Explaining what they need to know, showing how to do it. If I'm working for you, I want you to talk to me like I'm supposed to talk to you. I want you to treat me the same way I'm supposed to treat you.

Tom knew how to handle men, but he didn't have luck with his wife. He got separated from her. His wife was a nice looking woman, weighed about 140-150, just a nice size. She was living in town. He was living in the sugar mill quarters, where he worked during the week. He was crying. He got on his knees and begged her to come back. She wouldn't come back. That went on for months and months. So he finally give her up. When he give her up, then she wanted to come back, but he wouldn't let her. When he wouldn't take her back, she grieved herself to death and died. Just grieved herself to death; the saddest thing you would ever see. When she died she weighed very little. It made me feel so sad to watch that woman just grieving away like that.

We were all crazy about baseball. Even Clara was crazy about baseball. We didn't know nothing else but that. It was one of the few ways we could really enjoy ourselves. The only other fun was every Saturday night, something be happening at Meeker. There was always a dance going on, someone playing music—a guitar or something. There was always a little something to go to. People would cook up good food like fried fish or fried chicken and potato salad to sell. Clara's mother fried up good fish and chicken. Clara's mother used to make great cakes, too—all kinds—some with coconut, icings, jelly cakes. She used to do all the cakes by hand. She was a good cook. That's where Clara learned. We just had a nice time. We never been nowhere and know nothing else but that. We thought was nothing no better cause we ain't been nowhere else.

We had regular white uniforms. Times was tough, but I always managed to buy my own shoes. All the leagues wore the same kind of shoes. Now, you got all kinds of shoes. Then we all wore the same. When I wasn't pitching, I let somebody else wear my shoes. That's how tight it was.

When we traveled, we went in the back of a big truck that one of the people at the sawmill in Meeker let us use. We went through Louisiana to places like Lisbeth, Oakdale, and Rochelle, Selma and Goodpine, three sawmills way up there. We also played at Mansour, which is Creole land. That's a place that they live by theirselves. You ain't gonna see nobody there unless they're Creole. Our team went as far as Beaumont and Orange, Texas. We only played other Negro teams, never played whites. Along the way we'd stayed at little hotels or slept in the back of our truck when there was no place for blacks to stay. Sometimes we played on real baseball fields, but most of the time we played where there was nothing but pine woods, sawmills and good times. Whatever money we took in at the games got split between the players. We never made much, but it was something. We woulda played for nothing.

In the middle of a game, I would do the trick I taught myself. I'd put that ball in my heels, and throw it over head and grab it, run through the field with it. The people just laughed. I never saw nobody else do that trick. Nothing to it, after you learn it. Even later, when I worked on the waterfront in San Francisco, I would do the trick. I did it until I was fifty-five years old. When I got fifty-five I couldn't do it no more, I couldn't get the ball high enough. It hit me in the back.

During one game, I got hit in the front of my head and a knot come there, big as my head almost. I was so mad. I was just throwing the ball. I was crazy, I was so mad. I wasn't aiming to hit no one. I was throwing that ball around. I hit this guy and they had to take him out on a stretcher. I didn't mean to hit him. I was just mad, throwing the ball. When the game was over, my team had to get around me. All of them put me in the middle to keep the other team from jumping on me and beating me up. I didn't try to hit him. I was just mad.

I had a great time playing ball. But after I had played for about five years, I threw my arm away during a rainy day in Louisiana. I was pitching and a little shower came up. The day of this particular game it didn't rain that hard, but the rain wet the ball. I should never have been trying to curve the ball when it was wet. Nobody told me, "Don't curve the ball when it's wet." I was curving the ball and it wrecked my arm. Curving that wet ball just ruined my arm. I could never throw it hard no more.

I'm telling you, that was some kind of time. That was some kind of time. I think those were some of the happiest times in my life, playing baseball. I still love baseball.

People Thinks They's Free

◆

IN ABOUT 1925 I LEFT BOWMAN'S FARM AND WENT TO LIVE AT EMIL Jurett's. I had worked there when I still lived with my grandparents. He was a nice man to work for and I thought I could get a little more money there. I worked hard and, at first, earned more.

It rained harder in Louisiana than it rain here. Most of the time, when it was going to rain, you could see it from five miles away through the field. You be in the field working. You see the rain coming, way over, two or three miles. When you saw a storm coming, you'd run because storms were so strong, you'd get drowned before you could run fifty feet. That's how hard it rained. Rain just that hard in Louisiana. I can't figure out how the houses don't leak in the county. Maybe the tin roofs. Maybe the shingles. You never saw a house leak, don't care how hard it rained.

In 1927 there was a big flood. Right near Alexandria, the Red River was up to the top. The levees and dikes they had to keep the water back didn't work. There was too much water. The Red River and the Mississippi levees collapsed. They sent water all over. The river never got over as far as Meeker, so we didn't have to leave our homes, but the river was rising near Alexandria.

A bunch of us went from Meeker to Alexandria, eighteen miles away, to help work on the levee. Blacks and whites working together had something made like a wash bowl with two handles on it. The pail was about eighteen inches wide and two feet long. We'd fill it up with dirt and add the dirt to the levee. There was thousands of people packing dirt up there to make that levee; people was lined up, packing that dirt up there. That levee was pretty big, about twenty-five feet high, and about thirty feet wide. I remember the time we had walking up there with the dirt. The levee had to be kind of slanted so we could walk up there. If it hadn'ta been, you couldn'ta walked up there. No, no. When we worked, the water was just about three feet from the top of the levee and it was still rising.

From the top of the levee we could see over to the other side of the river where there was a big farming area. It was so far away that a man walking over there look just like a little boy. That river was just that high, right up to the top of the levee, and they didn't want anybody to go over to the other side and cut the levee to make the water go over there. People was scared to death somebody gonna cut that river. There were guys on both sides protecting their side of the river. They walk that river night and day so to be sure nobody wouldn't cut that levee. If somebody cut it, well, that's it, you could never stop it. The water was just that big. The water come up to the top. You see houses floating down the river. Chickens on a piece of wood. Dogs, cats on pieces of wood, floating down the river. You saw some of everything that you never saw before.

I liked working at Emil's, but after a few years I had to get away. I wasn't making nothing. When I left Bowman's I thought I make more money at Emil's. When I started there I did, but then I didn't. Emil Jurett was a man who like big times. He like baseball games. Everyday there's a game, he gonna park that horse by the store and get in a car with somebody, go on to Alexandria. That horse stayed tied there 'til he come back. When he get back to the farm, he find that the people who work for him done knocked off. Mr. Jurett kept going to ball games. He didn't take care of business. Later that's how he lost his farm, that way. I needed more money for my family. I told Clara that I ain't gonna borrow another mule. I was done with farming. I meant that.

When I left Emil's farm in 1928 or so, I went to work at a sawmill, the Felge Brothers Lumber Company in Lecompte, two miles from Meeker, closer to Lecompte. The sawmill was part of a big furniture company and I could make more money there. My job was stacking up lumber. That's where you made the money, stacking lumber. I made about forty-some dollars a week.

We had big quarters at the sawmill. There were a bunch of separate houses, eight or ten feet apart from each other. Each of the quarters had two rooms: a kitchen and a living room-bedroom. Most of the quarters didn't have no glass windows, only wooden doors to close and open. If you wanted any light in the house, you opened the doors, but there was no protection from anything. At some other quarters they had glass windows. When a worker moved out of a house with glass windows, I'd go there and take the windows from there, bring it and put it in my window space. Then when I wanted to see, I'd open the wooden window and see out of the glass window. No one in our quarter had windows like mine. I was the only one. I was always doing something to improve. I was a hustler that way.

We had a garden out back. Raised our vegetables and stuff. For awhile when things was real tough I bought some bootleg from a guy I knew. I took that bootleg and put it in some bottles and sold it. I'd hide them in the plants in the garden until I could sell it. Made a little extra to help out.

I didn't drink none—I sold it. I never really drank or smoked. When I was young and still living at my grandparents, I tried to smoke, but my grandma didn't want me to smoke. She say it weren't no good. So I just stopped. My parents didn't smoke or drink either. I never seen 'em take a drink or smoke or nothing. No. No.

When I was young, I used to see people get drunk, standing here and there and run to grab something to keep from falling down. And I said, "I know whiskey don't make nobody fall like that." I ain't never drank none, see. So one time I drank just to see would it make me do like that. I doing worse than they was. That learnt me a lesson right there. I don't want no more. I never drank again

Back then Clara and I were always able to live pretty good, even though money was tight. We grew whatever we needed. We only went to the store to get stuff like shortening or meal or flour, something like that. We raised most everything we ate—onions and mustard. Raised all them. Cabbage and sweet potatoes, too. In the summer we had delicious watermelon. Our garden always made life easier, especially when things got tough. That garden meant a whole lot. When we dug up sweet potatoes, Clara would make pie from the big ones, but we'd put smaller ones in the ashes from the fire to cook over night. In the morning they'd be soft and delicious. My wife was a good cook.

I had a way to keep the sweet potatoes fresh for a long time. I'd make a "tater pump." I learned how to build them from my daddy. First I built a pile of sweet potatoes about three feet high, in sort of a cone shape. I'd take the wagon and go out in the field to get some hay and corn stalks. I'd put the hay all around the potatoes to the ground, then put corn stalks on the hay. Then, I'd put dirt all the way to the top. I'd put an old tarp on the very top so it can't rain in there. The tarp didn't go all the way down the pump, but no matter how it rained, the potatoes all stayed dry. I never could figure that out. It look like the water would go in there, but it don't. It just run to the bottom.

In the tater pump the sweet potatoes stayed stored into the next year, never getting wet. Cold never kill them, or nothing. They stay right there until about time to start sprouting out. You just about eat all of 'em up about that time. Storing potatoes in the pump, we had potatoes almost all year.

Oh, them was some days, days I'll never forget as long as I live. Never. Meeker is just a little place there, but it's the first little place that I knowed anything about. Daddy and Mama lived in the country. Meeker, wasn't nothing there but two stores, the sugar mill and sawmill, but it was a town. There's plenty a people and that made it just nice. Sawmill quarters, sugar mill quarters, lots of people.

All the people in the sawmill quarters dealt with the big store owned by the sawmill or they deal with Hemingway's in Alexandria. That's a big store, a great big store. I never deal with the sawmill store or Hemingway's. People go to Hemingway, get stuff on credit; don't pay for that, go get something else, all on that same bill. They just kept on owing.

I ain't never go get that much at the store. I got something else going besides just depending on that store. I didn't go there and give them all my money. I didn't do that. I would go to Lecompte, about two miles away, and get anything I wanted. I got whatever I wanted, my bed and so forth, whatever I wanted. I go put things up and pay on it 'til I get it. When I brought it home, they's mine. I always bought stuff with cash, never on credit.

When the bossman says we gotta go slow cause it raining and we can't work, Clara and I didn't have no problems. With our garden, we don't be running to the store for everything. We didn't have to run to the store when work was slow. Some others ain't got nothing else going for them but the store. That's why they have to do that. If you go to the store, you kept owing and owing. When work was slow and men couldn't work, without a garden or fishing, you had nothing going for you but the store. A lot of people kept such a big bill at the store, if they wanted to leave, they couldn't cause they owed too much. People thinks they's free, but they weren't.

In 1929 the sawmill cut out, just stopped running. That's when times was tough. Herbert Hoover was in there. That's why the sawmill cut out; he stopped a lot of sawmills. I don't know how he stopped them, but he sure stopped them. He stopped a lot of other things, too. Hoover had the farmers plowing up the cotton, and starved the people to death. That's what made the Depression, when he was in there.

Our car was the only thing I lost during the Depression. When the sawmill cut out, we couldn't pay on the car no more. It was a year that I didn't pay the man. The man never said nothing about the car for the year. The tires kept wearing out. We kept getting flats. I didn't have the money to buy a new inner tube. So I patched it up and carried the car right down there where I bought it from. I got out of the car and went and gave the man the key. I said, "I just can't pay for it." He didn't say nothing. He knowed there wasn't no money. I didn't want to leave the car out somewhere and get it too dirty. I figured I could patch it some kind of way and get it to him. That's what I did.

That car was the only thing I lost; nothing else. All the people who had bought on credit lost everything. Two big trucks came and just cleaned the quarters out, took everything because the people owed them. Took everything that people had. People didn't have a bed to sleep in. Sleep on the floor.

I didn't do like they all did. I didn't try to keep up with them. I did like I wanted to. They should have had that paid for. But that's just trying to get more than you already got. You got to use your head for more than just a hat rack. Before the trucks came, they were laughing at me. After the trucks came, I was laughing at them cause I had a bed to sleep in and stuff in the house. I was laughing at them. I didn't lose nothing.

We survived all right because I was able to catch fish and make a garden. You got to think more than one way when things is scarce how to keep living. If all you know is to run to that store, you ain't gonna survive. I could always catch fish—perches and catfish especially.

In the summertime when the water was low, about three feet deep, a group of us would get a long net and stretch it across Bayou Boeuf, right along the edge of the water. Then a group of us would go way down there in the water by the bridge and beat the water. The fish would swim downstream into the net. We took the net up full of fish. Everybody got to eat fish when we did that. We get all of them fish out there, and divide them up between ourselves. Then we had plenty of fish to eat. We ate it up right away cause there was no way to keep it—no ice boxes or nothing.

Any Louisiana fish is real good, but there is nothing like eating a Louisiana perch. When Willie Mae weren't no more than two years old, she could already pick them bones out of the fish as good as any grown person. I still love Louisiana fish. There's a market near where I now live that gets fish from Shreveport, Louisiana—catfish and buffalo fish. I go get my fish there when I want to eat real good.

In 1929 when the sawmill cut out, I went to work at the nearby sugar mill, the Meeker Sugar Refinery; a great big sugar mill, a big, fine sugar mill where they grind cane. Sugar was big business. There was a lot sugar cane grown in Meeker. The Bowmans who owned Canebreak Farms, the one where I was, owned the mill. The Meeker Sugar Refining Company started just when I moved to my grandfather's. It was there for a long time. We still lived at the sawmill right across the road from the sugar mill. No one cared if we lived there. The sawmill was closed.

One of my jobs at the sugar mill was to operate the bull wheel, pulling the cane up from the bottom, carrying it up to the top so it could go right down the rollers. That was my job, just to sit right there and run the wheel. I could run it any speed I want, fast or slow, just keep it at a good speed to bring the cane up from the bottom to the top and the rollers and keep grinding the cane. The cane went through about five sets of rollers. The rollers get all the water, the juice, out of the cane. When it get to the last roller, it was dry. Grinding the cane start around the third of November and sometime we get through 'fore Christmas and sometime it be in January 'fore we get through.

Sometimes it got real cold in Louisiana. It got so cold that the ground was as hard as a rock, just freeze up. Sometimes it was so cold at the sugar mill, I can't ride the mule to get around. Walk on the ground and let the mule walk along with me. Had to walk to keep myself warmer. Sometimes when it was so cold, I would come home from work late at night. I would bring home some cane. Clara'd have the fire going, and I would peel cane and sit up and eat it with Clara and Willie Mae.

At the mill we always had a partner to work with, and a lot of time I worked with my brother George. Others worked seasons, but George and I had regular jobs at the mill, so we worked the whole year. When we were through grinding, the bossman always give us something to do. We did whatever the bossman needed. One year we painted the big shots' houses, inside and out. One year I worked with a black pipe fitter named Frank

Wills. You couldn't make nobody no better than him. He was great. Nothing could come up there that he couldn't fix. He might work pipe this year and next year operate the crane near the train, moving cars back and forth. Frank taught me how to fit pipe real good.

Frank used to be a "houseman." If you were a houseman, you had to know how to do everything. That's what a houseman means. And Frank could do it. If he's in his bed asleep and something go wrong, someone go get him out of the bed and he go there and fix whatever. No matter what, he knew how to fix it.

The sugar mill had its own train. Something was wrong with it. Frank worked fixing the train engine. It take Frank about three months to tear it down and put it back. The first time he did it, it would run forwards, but wouldn't run backwards. Frank tore it back down, went in there again, built it up. When he put it back together that time, they had no problem. He had nothing to do but that, so he could take his time.

The depression hit Louisiana bad. The sawmill was closed. The sugar mill started to have problems too. There was nothing else in Meeker to do, no way to make money. One time I walked 28 miles, right from Meeker to Oakdale, Louisiana, to find work. Oakdale was in sawmill country. Nan's son, Willie, was living out there workin at the sawmill that wasn't shut down. There were a lot of sawmills in Louisiana and they didn't all close down in the Depression. I stayed with Willie and worked at the sawmill about a month to get some money. Then I come back and start cutting cane or whatever, farming. Just that three or four weeks of work at the sawmill helped a whole lot.

At Oakdale, they was working to put them logs on the train, bringing them down to the river. They attached a cable to a tree, then loaded logs onto the train. I wouldn't do that. I know how dangerous it was. Putting the log on the tongs, taking the logs over trees, the logs keep going. They ain't gonna stop until they get on the train cars. A freight train for logs had about twelve or fifteen cars of logs. The log train is kinda of tilted like, and when the train get to the river, they take that chain loose and the logs run right in the water.

After the logs were in the water, they stay in the log pool. There are two men in the pool with log sticks and they shove the logs and hook them right on there and pull them right up to the mill. Then they take the cable off it and saw the logs.

Then they start the sawing. It's just amazing to see how a sawmill work. The sawyer has two levers and he see right down there where the glider set the logs. He twists the log and knows just what to set it on. The sawyer runs a great big band saw, about fifteen feet long. He cuts the log and every time he cuts the log, the log falls over. The sawyer uses another part of the machine and turns the big log, like it was a toothpick or something. He cuts another side of the log. He cuts the whole log like that, get it shaped like he want to about ten or twelve inches squared. He carries it back over to a gang of saws, each just an inch apart, and cut that wood into planks at one time.

After the sawyer gets done, the wood goes right down to the edger. He cut it and make it even. The bark part go one way and the wood the other. Right out at the end, the bark and scrap goes down into a big hole where they burn what they don't want. The hole was about twenty feet below. The fire burnt year round. Rain don't put it out. It could rain all day, all night, never puts it out. It's too big a fire. You don't see the fire, but it's down in there.

When the lumber was cut and ready to go, they got a dock with cross ties. They lay the lumber on the cross ties, down at the end. Then you make the cross ties loose and slide the lumber right on the train car. It's just amazing just to look at it and see how it works.

This guy I knew wanted to get me a job out there, but I didn't want it. I turned it down. I couldn't live there. Too many guys get hurt out there. Just too rough. Shooting up everybody. Every month somebody get killed at that sawmill. Quarter bosses walked the quarters night and day to try and keep the people settled down and keep the fighting from going on. But still, there was always someone getting killed. It was just too rough. I couldn't live there with my family.

One time, me and two guys were standing out there, back of the row of housing, talking. A woman start to walk along. I didn't know who she was, just some woman walking along. She had on an apron. This other woman was walking towards her. When the woman in the apron got close to the second woman, she shot the woman right through her apron. The apron hid her gun. The shot hit the second woman in her thigh. The bullet went on through. The woman didn't even know she was shot and kept on walking. The woman in the apron turned around and broke and run. That place was just too rough—things like that happening all the time.

When I was at Oakdale, there was this guy living right next door to me.

I don't know whether he was working or not, but I was working. He was going over to Meeker and I give him $3.50 to take back to Clara. Back then $3.50 was a lot of money. He didn't give it to her. He made like somebody robbed it. How could a guy do something like that? Say somebody robbed him. Took the money and spend it himself. Living next door, I just knowed he gonna give it to her. But I was wrong. That's just how some people are.

When we could we still played baseball. One day in 1932 when my baby brother, Henry, was eighteen, he was running to first base during a game. A guy threw the ball to try to get him out and the ball hit Henry on the back of the head. Henry seemed okay so we didn't pay it too much mind.

Henry must have got some kind of infection, because after awhile there was fluid coming out of his ears. We didn't know. He didn't want it running out of his ears, so he put cotton in them. He tried to keep it hid. He didn't want anybody knowing. The knot and the infection stayed there awhile. When I learned about it, I took him to one of the doctors in Lecompte. I think it was Dr. Hardy. The doctor examined him. He didn't give me no information about him getting worse or better or nothing.

He didn't get better, so I got some money together and sent Henry to a hospital in New Orleans, about three hundred miles away. I couldn't go with him because we didn't have enough money for both of us to go. I thought that he'd get well there and come on back.

On the ninth day after he went to the hospital I got a telegram telling me that he died that morning around ten o'clock. We didn't have the money to bring him back home. He's buried somewhere in New Orleans. There was no money ... no money ... no money ....

INTERLUDE

❧

As Mr. Wilson and I worked together, my curiosity about the places and times he spoke of grew. Initially I just wanted to know more about Bunkie, Meeker and Negro baseball. But as he continued with his story, I became equally interested in Galveston and San Francisco during the 30's and 40's. I began by reading books about Louisiana, both fiction and non-fiction. Ernest Gaines' writings, particularly *A Lesson Before Dying* and *A Gathering of Old Men,* gave me a clearer sense of what it felt like being a black man in Louisiana. I could easily picture Mr. Wilson as one of the older men on Mathu's porch in *A Gathering of Old Men.* I also learned to do research on the Internet, which proved more successful than I had expected, not so much in the information I learned directly there, but the people and addresses it led me to, most notably Betty Williams, the librarian in the Bunkie library. As I learned more about the times and places in which Mr. Wilson lived, I was beginning to feel like a detective. Sometimes it seemed the more I learned, the more questions I had.

Mr. Wilson's story begins in Bunkie, a small delta town in Avoyelles Parish, a rural area in the center of Louisiana. There was, and still is, little in the parish aside from the bayous and the good farmland surrounding them. Of Avoyelles' 534,000 acres, 462,290 are fertile soil deposited by the flowing waters of the rivers and bayous. Avoyelles continues to have virtually no urban population at all.[iv]

Initially the town of Bunkie was called Irion after Major Irion, a veteran of the War of 1812, who first settled in the area in 1822. Sixty years later, when the Texas & Pacific Railway needed the right of way for its rail line, they approached Captain Samuel Haas (pronounced Hays) for the land they needed. Captain Haas, a Civil War veteran and the largest landowner in the area, agreed to give the railroad the land in return for which he was given the honor of naming the station and by default, naming the town. The captain decided to name the station after his daughter Maccie. After a fashion he did.

When Maccie was a young child, just beginning to talk, she was given a pet monkey. She was so young that she couldn't pronounce the letter "m" correctly, and consequently called her pet "Bunkie." Over time, Bunkie became not only the monkey's name, but Maccie's nickname, as well as the town's name.[v] Bunkie was and continues to be a small town. In 1990, Bunkie, the second largest town in Avoyelles Parish, had only 5,044 inhabitants.

As helpful as it was to read about Louisiana history, visiting was better. In the spring of 1998, my husband and I were invited to the wedding of young friends, Caren Mayer and Nick Orem, in Baton Rouge. Caren had already been helpful in my search when she connected me with her father, Jim, who still lives in Louisiana. Jim provided good counsel in my search for official papers. The invitation to Caren and Nick's wedding gave me a second reason to go to Louisiana and we jumped at the chance.

My husband, Alan, and I flew into Alexandria late one evening in May 1998 and began the following day by stopping for breakfast at Lea's Lunchroom in LeCompte. Located between the northbound and southbound lanes of U.S. 71 at a highway crossing south of Alexandria, Lea's has been at the same location since 1928. On one of the walls, a motto is engraved in wood: "He who enters here is a stranger but once." Soon I understood why the motto was on the wall.

After the waitress had taken our orders of eggs, biscuits and grits, my husband told her that I was working on the oral history of a man from the area and wondered if there was anyone around who knew some of local history.

"Mr. Smith knows a fair bit," she said over her shoulder as she wandered off. We had no idea who Mr. Smith was or if he were one of the many men eating in the restaurant. When she returned with our food, she said, "Mr. Smith'll talk to you. He's over there," as she pointed to a table where three men sat.

I walked over, still having no idea who Mr. Smith was, and introduced myself to the trio at the table. One of the men stood up and shook my hand. At 6 feet, he was as tall and straight as Mr. Wilson, though not as old. R. B. Smith came back with me to our table. He had grown up in LeCompte and was now retired as principal of the local high school. He told us about the farms, sugar mill and saw mill that had been in Meeker and bemoaned the loss. The sawmill closed in the late 1920's and the sugar mill in 1981. Both mills had been central to the local economy for many years, and without them, the area now relied solely on agriculture. When I asked him more about the sawmill and sugar mill, he offered to show us where they were. As we followed Mr. Smith's car, the land of Mr. Wilson's youth came alive.

Today, there is no Meeker to speak of. On a map Meeker appears as two intersecting streets, but it is difficult to see where there had been any town at all. When Mr. Wilson moved there in 1916, Meeker had a sawmill, sugar refinery, general store and a post office. Today, only the skeleton of the sugar refinery remains. The site where the sawmill once operated, across the road from the sugar mill, is now corn fields. Mr. Smith then took us to LeCompte where we visited the Chamber of Commerce and purchased a book about the local history. We thanked him and continued on our way to Bunkie.

Many of the buildings mentioned by Mr. Wilson remain in Bunkie. The Merchants' and Planters' Bank, where John Rhodes was an assistant cashier (a position similar to assistant manager) sits in the middle of Main Street, its site since 1900 when it opened in a town of 873 people. William D. Haas, a descendent of Samuel, the founder of Bunkie, owned the bank.[vi] The bank was closed in 1934 and the building has had several reincarnations since then, including that of a restaurant, operated by Lea's daughter (as in Lea's Lunchroom) before the Cottonport Bank opened in 1998.

The train station is a half block from the bank, but we were unable to find any path over the bayou and, in fact, couldn't find the bayou in town. Prior to our visit, I had tried to locate a deed of ownership for Mr. Wilson's father's farm, but despite my best attempts, I was unable find any record of the senior John Wilson owning a farm. The parish clerk did not respond to letters or phone calls. With the way over the bayou hidden and no deed or address, we couldn't find the farm lived on by the Wilson family, which was a great disappointment.

After we wandered a bit through Bunkie, we went to the library located off Main Street on Oak Street. Betty Williams, the librarian, was most welcoming and helpful. Although we had never met, we had spent much time on the phone, and it felt as if we knew each other. Mrs. Williams was as helpful in person as she had been over the phone. She referred me to local historians, calling first to make a personal connection and then took me to meet Cici Ducote at the Chamber of Commerce, who she thought might be of help. Although Ms. Ducote was busy preparing for the Louisiana Corn Festival to be held in Bunkie in June, she took the time to answer my questions. Mrs. Williams also directed us to one of the cemeteries where Mr. Wilson's parents might be buried.

We left the library and headed to the cemetery, adjacent to the Second Union Baptist Church which was easy to find with Mrs. Williams' directions. Although we found the cemetery, we were not able to find John Wilson's grave. There were no headstones in the cemetery. A man at the church explained that there was nothing written that told where specific graves were located. There had been one man in the congregation who knew the history of the cemetery, but he too had died.

Further down the road, we found the church in Eola that Mr. Wilson had described where they "rang tone in the bell" when someone died. The bell was still on the ground next to the steeple, where it had fallen during a storm many years before.

The trip to Louisiana, though brief, gave me a greater sense of the area. At one point in Bunkie, Alan and I were standing in front of the library, looking towards the train station. A woman came out of a store and stared at us for a few minutes. Her expression was not friendly. I went over to her, introduced myself, and told her I why we were visiting. Her attitude changed instantaneously. Once she knew of my interest in the town's history, she began telling us with pride about the other buildings that were in the town in the early part of the century. I had a clear sense of both the simultaneous distrust and the welcoming of strangers.

With Mrs. Williams and Mr. Smith's help, I located several books on the local history. Reading and researching the history of the local area as well as about the reconstructionist South gave me a greater understanding of the times in which Mr. Wilson lived. At the time of his childhood, the South had settled into post-Reconstruction. In Louisiana, as elsewhere in the South, whites and blacks had clearly defined roles. While slavery had been legally abolished, servitude had not. Most blacks, particularly in rural areas like Avoyelles, Bunkie's parish, were sharecroppers, farm workers or otherwise worked for whites in some manner. Few had any financial independence.

Despite his son's memories, John Wilson Sr. may never have owned a farm, and rather, may have rented through the bank. According to the 1910 census, John Wilson was renting a farm in April of that year, the year Mr. Wilson thought his father bought the farm. Whether he actually owned or rented, he was still in a very small group of black men who did not work directly for whites. In the South, black land ownership was rare. In 1910, there were 12,039 African-Americans living in the Avoyelles Parish, 27.9% of the population. Of that number, 862 black men rented and 100 owned farms. Generally, the few who rented their land had relatively small acreage.[vii]

As unusual as it was for a black man to own a farm, it was even more extraordinary for a black man to own a farm the size described by Mr. Wilson. The array of crops, animals, and the number of people working for him attest to John Wilson's success. With the success came potential danger. In the South at that time, the mere appearance of a comfortably situated black man placed that man and his family in a precarious position.

Mr. Wilson's question about why Mr. Rhodes would help his father buy a farm is intriguing to me. Sometimes when black men bought land, they did so with the assistance of whites. While there were any number of reasons a white man might help a black man, Mr. Wilson had no insight as to why Mr. Rhodes, or Mr. Rhodes acting for Mr. Haas, was helpful aside from how his father "dealt with him." It's also curious that Mr. Wilson's mother and remaining brothers were able to stay on the farm for the year until Mrs. Wilson died. She was too ill to work and the people who had worked for his father had left. With no one to farm there was no income to pay the rent or mortgage, yet the family stayed.

John Wilson died on May 20, 1915 at the age of 37. The death certificate, with John Rhodes signing as the "informant," states that the cause of death was tuberculosis, although his son has no recollection of his father coughing, only that he was weak. No doctor visited John Wilson while he was sick. There is an obvious discrepancy between

Mr. Wilson's memory and the death certificate. For the purposes of his life story, the "real story," which we will never know, is less important than Mr. Wilson's belief that his father was poisoned. He lived his life with that belief, making the belief his reality.

Mr. Wilson's mother, Siphronia died almost one year later, on March 24, 1916. Her death certificate, signed by her father-in-law, Philip Wilson, states that she, like her husband, had died of consumption. Mr. Wilson's recollection of what his aunt and uncle had said was that she had an ulcer.

While there is no proof that Mr. Wilson's parents, his sisters, and brother were murdered, it is quite probable. Successful blacks were a threat to white supremacy. In John Wilson's case, not only did he have a successful farm, but a white man had been evicted from the property so that the Wilson's family could live there. This act would not have been taken lightly. While I didn't find it surprising that members of the Wilson family were poisoned, it did surprise me that they hadn't been killed sooner or in a more violent way, given that a conservative estimate of the number of blacks lynched between 1890 and 1917 was between two and three per week.[viii]

The more Mr. Wilson told his story, the more questions I had, most of which can never be answered. In addition to the questions concerning the farm ownership and the deaths of his parents and siblings, I was curious about his grandparents, particularly his grandfather. Mr. Wilson was thirteen in 1916 when he left Bunkie and moved north to Meeker, an antebellum plantation community in Rapides Parish, to live on his grandparents' farm. Much as with Bunkie, the area around Meeker was largely agricultural. Cotton, corn and sugar cane were the major farm products of the area. Forest areas around the farmland provided timber for the lumber industry.

Mr. Wilson knew little about his grandparents. He assumed they were slaves, given what he supposed their ages were, but didn't know for sure. Through the 1900 and 1910 United States census, I was able to learn a bit, but not much. Looking through microfilmed census data is tedious work. Initially I had been searching for some idea of the numbers of black men who owned or rented farms in either Avoyelles or Rapides Parishes. As I looked, I noted the names, looking for any of Mr. Wilson's relatives.

Suddenly, as I scanned the 1900 census from Avoyelles Parish, I realized that I was looking at a listing for Phillip Wilson, Johnnie's grandfather, and his family. I had not expected to find Phillip Wilson in the Avoyelles census because I had not been aware that he had lived there. By the time their grandson, Johnnie, knew them, they lived in Rapides Parish. When I saw the information about Phillip Wilson, I felt as if I had found a pot of gold. In the 1900 census, months and years of individual's births were listed. This was no longer the case in 1910. Thus, I was able to learn that Phillip Wilson was born in April 1852 in Louisiana, and that Lutisha was born in March 1860, also in Louisiana. Mr. Wilson's grandparents had indeed been born before the Civil War, and in all likelihood had been slaves, although they were not as old as their grandson thought.

In 1900, Phillip, Lutisha, their four sons, John, Clifton, Philip and Coleman, along with Coleman's wife, Sophronia, rented a farm in Avoyelles Parish.[ix] By 1920, Philip owned a farm in Rapides Parish.[x] The reason the family left the farm they rented in Avoyelles and bought one in Rapides is unknown. Phillip Wilson's ability to rent and then own a farm is even more impressive, particularly when, according to his grandson, he had no help in the fields. That, added to his seemingly unprovoked hostility towards the white man walking through his land, was potentially dangerous, not only to himself, but to anyone living in his home. It is perplexing that he got away with it.

Another question about Phillip Wilson that will never be answered is why he so mistreated his grandson. According to Mr. Wilson, his grandfather was both physically abusive and distant from him. At that time, physical punishment was not unusual in many families, black or white. It was one way for parents to make certain that their children learned right from wrong. Black parents in particular had to be sure that their children knew how to survive in the South. If black children or, for that matter, black adults were not deferential to whites, it could cost them their lives.[xi] There was no room for mistakes. Black parents tried to teach their children to demonstrate proper respect for all adults, first within their own family, then for the larger black community and finally towards whites. Only when their children were routinely respectful to their black elders, could their parents feel more certain that they would also act appropriately subordinate to whites. Lorrel, Mr. Wilson's grandson-in-law, who grew up in Texas, remembers his grandfather saying, "I'll keep you in line before the white man kills you."

Given Johnnie Wilson's thoughts about his grandfather's "meanness," it's curious that Phillip Wilson even considered sending him to school. The little we know about Phillip would point to his believing that physical work, not education, was the way to get ahead.

Education, as with most other issues involving blacks in the South, was not simple. In some ways education ranked very high in esteem for many black families. Literacy had been denied to slaves and the pursuit of education was one of the great luxuries equated with freedom. On the other hand, being too educated could bring trouble. An educated black man might question or, in some less direct way, show that he knew as much or more than a white man. Knowing how to write, when many whites could not, could make a black man seem "above his proper station." As with the appearance of prosperity, the appearance of being educated could lead to difficulties with whites. While black leaders saw education as a way to success, in the South it was another threat to white supremacy and therefore a danger to blacks.

Phillip Wilson considered sending Johnnie to school, to the point of buying him new clothes. Had his grandfather not listened to the traveling fortunetellers, Johnnie might have achieved the beginnings of school learning. There were some schools for blacks in the Bunkie and Meeker area that Johnnie could have attended. Children who did attend schools could do so only when they weren't needed in the fields. In 1915, in Avoyelles Parish, the average length of the school year for black children was three months. Even with such a short school term, only forty percent of school-aged African-American children attended school that year.[xii] Without the help of every member of the family, it was almost impossible for families to survive. Phillip Wilson needed Johnnie in the fields.

Mr. Wilson thought that his father and uncles had been to school. According to the information given to the census taker, they probably had not.[xiii] None of them could read, at least not that they admitted to the census taker. His father, John, could write and his mother, Siphronia, could both read and write.

Mr. Wilson never stopped trying to improve his reading and writing. His granddaughter, Betty, remembers him frequently asking her how to spell words. "He'd be reading the newspaper. He always read the sports section. If he didn't know a word, he'd skip over it, go on, then come back to it. He'd get an idea of what the word was. Then he'd ask me how to spell what he thought it was. Once I'd spell it for him, he knew he was right." He was as patient with his writing as he was with his reading. He'd take his time, get everything in order and write precisely what he meant to. Because it took him a long time to write, he might write part of a letter on one day and then return to it the following day.

As I thought about Mr. Wilson's deep respect for learning and his ongoing pursuit of literacy, I was reminded of my father, Teddy, who had been born two years before Mr. Wilson in Satu Mare, Hungary, now a part of Romania. Although he had received a basic education, he was not able to continue his formal learning. Gymnasiums, which offered higher education, accepted very few Jews. When he came to the United States in 1920, he had to support himself and didn't have the luxury of going back to school. Instead he became a beautician and, with my mother, ran a beauty salon for almost thirty years. My father didn't enjoy his work any more than Mr. Wilson enjoyed unloading gravel, but did what was needed to support his family.

Much like Mr. Wilson, my father was a self-taught man. He read continuously, particularly history, and respected those with advanced education. Like my father, I have always loved to read. As Mr. Wilson and my father knew, reading is, in many ways, a key to being able to move ahead in the world. My work with Mr. Wilson reinvigorated my commitment to literacy. I have, in recent years, combined my social work training with my desire to strengthen literacy by serving on the board of the San Francisco Head Start and tutoring through the Jewish Coalition for Literacy, both programs that help ensure that children will learn to read.

As Mr. Wilson well recognized, with more education, he could have had a different life. He thought that with better reading and writing skills, he could have been a walking boss on the waterfront. I think with his intelligence, he would have gone way beyond the waterfront. At the very least, his patience and ongoing efforts to learn set an example for his family. When Mr. Wilson taught himself to read and write, he set new expectations for the generations to follow him.

Mr. Wilson also passed his love of baseball to his family. When he was first involved with the sport, baseball was just becoming a national pastime. Black men, who could not play on white teams, instead formed their own. In addition to the official Negro League, there were many semi-pro teams playing throughout the country. Mr. Wilson and the Meeker Dirty Devils were a part of such a group of semi-pro teams. In Mr. Wilson's area, his team and others were composed of men who lived and worked together. Games were usually held only in the evenings or on weekends when the men were not needed at work. Whenever and wherever they could, they played. While his team shared whatever they earned, it is not likely that they earned much after paying for gas and other travel expenses. They were in it for love, not money.

By the time I was a young child, baseball was integrated. I didn't realize the significance of Jackie Robinson, other than my brother, Richie, thought he was a great player. Richie loved baseball. He loved listening to it and watching it. He still does. In high school he played first base and left field on a local team called the Astoria Braves. We often went to games to watch him. He was six years older than I, and, consequently, I spent a good deal of time watching baseball games. I also grew up in a neighborhood where both girls and boys played stick-ball. While I showed no talent at the game, it was a fun way to spend summer evenings. When Lorrel told me that it would help if I knew something about baseball, I could honestly say I did.

While I did know something about baseball, I knew virtually nothing about Negro baseball, other than that black men who weren't able to play the game with white men, formed their own teams. I contacted Peter Rutkoff, Director of the American Studies Program at Kenyon College, where both my husband and oldest daughter, Sara, went to college. When Sara was there, she had taken a class from Peter called "Baseball and American Culture" and had researched Larry Doby, the man who integrated the American League by joining the Cleveland Indians 1947. As I expected, Peter steered me in the right direction, toward a book entitled *Only the Ball Was White* by Robert Peterson.

When Mr. Wilson first told me about and, despite his advanced years, tried to demonstrate the trick he did with the baseball, I had no idea what a trick such as his had to do with baseball. As Peterson explains, in the earlier years, baseball was as much a social occasion and form of entertainment as it was an athletic exhibition. Many players had routines they included while they played. They might juggle the ball or use acrobatics to throw or catch, or a player might hit the ball and run the bases in reverse order. For players and spectators alike, baseball provided a change from the daily routine in more ways than one. Part of the joy of the game for Mr. Wilson, and I suspect for many other players, was the good times they were able to give their spectators. This love was still evident when Mr. Wilson spoke of and demonstrated his baseball skills. He passed his love of baseball on to younger generations of his family, as evidenced by his great-grandson, Lorrel Jr's, continued attendance at Giants' opening-day games. Lorrel is called Scoop by his family and Yogi by his grandfather, after Yogi Berra.

Mr. Wilson also showed great pride in his ability to support his family within the constraints of being a black man in the South. From his father and, in some ways, from his grandfather as well, Mr. Wilson learned at an early age to keep himself focused on making his life better. He never outwardly bucked the system, but maneuvered within it to improve his conditions. He was able to see pitfalls and work around them.

One of these pitfalls, clearly recognized by Mr. Wilson, was the company store. Storekeepers on plantation-type farms or industry often exploited the illiteracy and imposed subservience of the workers. No matter how hard blacks worked, they were never able to get ahead. When it came time to settle up after a harvest, black farmers always seemed to owe more than they had earned, starting each new year in debt. If a tenant farmer or worker wanted to move, he couldn't until the debt to the store was paid off, which, given the power of the storekeepers, never happened. Since most blacks were unschooled, they had to accept the accounting as given by the storeowner. Even with education, it was not wise to question. Dealing with plantation stores kept blacks in another form of slavery. As Mr. Wilson so clearly states, "People think they's free, but they weren't."

Mr. Wilson never fell into this pattern. He grew his own vegetables at home, fished, stored sweet potatoes and went to the store as seldom as possible. Although he didn't drink alcohol, he stored moonshine to sell. He was able to do this without drawing undue attention to his independence. The fact that Mr. Wilson was able to work around the system speaks to his ingenuity and diligence, skills that served him equally well as he moved on.

My family did not have the depth of struggle that Mr. Wilson and his family did, but, we were, to say the least, not wealthy. The beauty salon that my parents ran was only moderately successful, and there was little left over for extras. Money was always a worry, particularly for my father. Nothing was wasted. We had goulash soup as often as goulash.

Much as Johnnie and Clara Wilson, my parents did everything that needed to be done around the house. I don't remember ever having anyone come to fix anything. Painting, wall papering, upholstery, drapes, plumbing, electrical work, my parents did it all. My mother made most of my clothes, and although she was an excellent seamstress, I remember not appreciating her talent. I wanted store bought clothes like the kids at school wore. Only as I grew older did I fully appreciate the gift my mother had for sewing and knitting. I once brought home a corduroy blazer from Bloomingdale's. I knew it was unlikely I could keep it, but thought it was worth a try. As I expected, my mother said it was too expensive and that I would have to return it the following Saturday. By the time Saturday came, my mother, sewing in the evenings after work, had made me an exact copy of the jacket.

My parents' skills served them well. It allowed them to fulfill the dreams they had when they moved to the United States. Although Johnnie and Clara Wilson used all the tools at their disposal to improve their lives, they lived in a culture that tried to keep them subservient. They never accepted that definition of themselves. They continually sought ways to better their lives. Leaving Louisiana offered such a chance.

The "big church" in Eola, near Bunkie,
with the "tone in the bell" beside.

Johnnie's grandparents,
Phillip and Luticia Wilson.

The old Felge Brothers Lumber Company sawmill in Lecompte, near Meeker.

The old Meeker Sugar Refinery.

Clara, circa 1947.

Johnnie

Johnnie, Clara and Betty, San Francisco, 1946.

Betty and Lorrel at Johnnie's 95th.

*Trina and Willie Mae at Johnnie's
95th birthday, June 1998.*

To Be a Man

AFTER MY BABY BROTHER HENRY DIED IN '32, I JUST GOT DISGUSTED about living in Louisiana and having nothing. Things were real slow … no work. Work didn't start picking up in the area until 1935 or 1936. Roosevelt had the W.P.A. where they helped the people. He had them cutting down trees on Bayou Boeuf just to give people work. That was a big help. That's how things finally started picking up. But before that people were leaving Louisiana looking for other places where they could work. You had to try and go somewhere, try to find something, cause there's nothing there. I thought about going somewhere else.

We didn't know nothing about any other place. But if you got to go, you find somewhere to go. You just set out, go places until you can find a better place. That's what we did. I thought about my brother Coleman and Clara's brother, Clarence Reed, in Galveston, Texas and in 1934 I finally decided to go join them.

When I left Meeker I didn't owe that man in the store nothing. When I left there, I wasn't scared to go back because I didn't owe nobody nothing. No, no. I take care of business. That's something I learned from my father. He never had to borrow nothing from nobody. I grow up just in his footsteps. Other people didn't have nothing. For everything they had to do, had to borrow someone's wagon. My daddy had his own wagon and a buggy. Never had to borrow.

I took a freight train with my half-brother, Monk. Back then people took freight trains to get around. If you didn't know how to ride freight trains, you had to walk everywhere you go. Most of us didn't have trucks or cars, only our feet. I'd ride freight trains all the time when I go somewhere, just like I leave home to go two miles to town, I'd wait til the freight train pass, catch that freight train and ride that freight train to town. If I didn't, I'd have to walk. People were even riding freight trains with their babies. You know it's tough when people do that.

I learned how to ride freight trains during the Depression. You had to learn just how to catch a train because you could get hurt or killed if you didn't do it right. You had to jump onto the train when it was going thirty-five to forty miles an hour. Learning it wasn't easy. You learn first when a train was running slow, like when it done passed a station and start off running ten, fifteen, twenty miles; that's how you learn, at a slow speed. You had to be strong to pull yourself up even at the slow speeds. As you go along, you learn more and more. You can catch it going more faster. After you learned to ride them, there was nothing to it.

Monk and I went to Alvin, Texas, a town about 25 miles from Galveston and 25 miles from Houston. That's where Nolan Ryan lives. The town was real small. Back then, it had only about one store. When the sun began to get low and it began to get late, I said, "Monk, we better get away from here cause I ain't seen nary a black person." I wanted to get away from there before it get dark. I didn't want to be in that small town after dark. I was afraid. You don't know what they do to you. You just couldn't take no chances in staying where they was after the sun go down. So me and him just started walking to Galveston even though we didn't know exactly how far it was then. Finally we got lucky and got a ride. We found Clarence in Galveston and stayed with him for awhile.

The hard thing about going to Galveston was that Clara and Willie Mae had to stay behind in Louisiana. I couldn't bring them to live with me until I could earn some money to take care of them. They stayed with Clara's mother, Lutishie. Lutishie still lived on the Bowman farm. She had ten children of her own and always had somebody else's children at the house too. She liked having Clara and Willie Mae stay with her.

While she was there, Clara worked in the kitchen at Bowman's farm so she was gone most of the day. She earned extra money sewing clothes for white people on an old treadle machine. Clara sewed real well. Clara did a lot of things well. Willie Mae used to sit under the sewing machine and press the treadle to make the machine run when Clara sewed. Clara made all their clothes. Sometimes she washed flour and potato sacks real good and used them for Willie Mae's underwear and dresses. She'd bleach them out and make real pretty things out of them. Back then they had pretty flour sacks.

When I got to Galveston I saw it was a nice seaport town. Anywhere you go you see water cause it's surrounded by water. There's a lot of shipping there. You can't get there unless you cross water some way. You can cross on a ferry or a bridge. In the winter it gets cold. There's ice on the ground. In the summer it gets real hot. All year long you hear the waves at night. Hear them big waves coming in, the waves coming in hit them big rocks. When you first moved there, you wasn't used to them.

Clarence, Clara's brother, worked at W. D. Hayden, a large construction supply company with places in Galveston, Port Arthur and Houston. They had a great big place in Houston. Hayden had ships that went out to get shell deposits and sand. The city used the shell when they fixed the streets. They used the sand in cement and stuff. In Galveston, Hayden was right in the middle of the city.

Clarence made me change my name to Johnnie Reed, so it seem like I was his brother. That way he could help me get a job easier where he worked. I was Johnnie Reed for a good while. At first I rode around town with Clarence when he was at work so I could learn the town. The boss-man, Mr. Tucker, liked me and give me little jobs to do, like cutting somebody's yard or something. Mr. Tucker was a nice boss. Work finally picked up and I got a more permanent job at Hayden's material yard, where I did just about everything. They bought a brand new truck for me to drive to haul bricks and different things.

My brother, Coleman, was working at another place when I first got to Galveston. Clarence brought him there when he was sixteen. He didn't have a regular job, but after I got out there, that's what made him start working at Hayden too. Our nephew, Perry, was in Galveston too. I knowed Perry since he was about seven or eight years old when me and Clara was going together. He's Clara's sister, Viola's, son. We had a lot of family in Galveston.

Once I got the job at Hayden, I was able to save a little bit of money and get a place of my own. As soon as I had enough money, I went back to Louisiana to get Clara and Willie Mae. Willie Mae was about seven years old then. It took me just about a year and a half to go back for my family.

Clarence had this car with one rumble seat behind the driver. He drove me back to Louisiana to get them. The car sure was crowded on the way back to Galveston. There was no trunk for their clothes and such. It only had one seat up front. The drive took about four or five hours.

When Clara and Willie Mae first came, we lived with Clarence. Coleman and his wife, Viola, were also living there. Then Coleman and we got a place and sent for George and his wife. We all lived on 33rd and H, on the corner of the alley. We could hear the waves at night from our house. It was a good size house. It had three bedrooms. You come in the house and there's a hall there. To the right was Coleman's bedroom and on the left was George's. At the end of the hall was a door that went into the living room and kitchen. On the left of the kitchen was another hall and it led to my bedroom and the bathroom. You use the hall to get to the bathroom. Didn't have to go through my bedroom. We didn't have a garden so we hustled around and got things from the little shops that sold greens like mustard and onions and different things.

Our three families got along just fine living in the same house. We had to get along to live in the same house together. Each family had our own bedroom and we shared the kitchen. We gave Coleman the biggest bedroom. He liked that. Everybody cooked for themselves. Sometimes we'd end up in the kitchen eating together, but it wasn't planned that way. We never had no problems.

Coleman and George loved kids, but they never had none. They just didn't worry about it. That was the way it was. Monk got married. He didn't have no kids neither. Willie Mae was the only child in the family, so she got a lot of attention. They was crazy about Willie Mae. She was still Willie Mae then. She had so many names. Her mother called her "Turtle Baby." I didn't like "Turtle Baby," so I called her "Puddin." Coleman called her "Boo." Now most people call her Tillie. Willie Mae was as fine as she could be. We never had no trouble with her.

When Willie Mae first came to Galveston, she was real small and slept with us in our bed. When she got older, we didn't want her in our bed no more and moved a bed into the big hall for her. She didn't like to sleep there, so after we went to bed, she'd come into our room and get on the foot of our bed and go back to sleep. Later she did get used to sleeping in her own bed. Our cat and dog slept in the bed with her. They kept her company. We'd go past her bed to see three little heads laying in a row. I sure wish I'd a taken a picture of that.

Willie Mae was always a sickly child. She would have high fevers and all, real high temps. When she got older, she stopped being so sick. Her doctor never told her anything specific, but him and the Lord cured her. She never took nothing for it. It just went away. Have no idea what it was.

When Willie Mae came to Galveston, she was behind for her age in school. She had the age, but not the learning. They had to put her back cause she hadn't been taught. When Willie Mae went to school in Meeker, there were at least fifteen children at the school for the younger kids. I think the older kids went to another school. The teacher, she didn't do nothing but sit Willie Mae on the desk. She didn't teach her anything. She just had her sitting there. I guess she was too small. I can't remember if she went back into kindergarten or the first grade when she got to Galveston.

Some Spanish people lived near our house. One of the girls was around Willie Mae's age, and they all played together. Their mother couldn't speak English. The kids would trade food. They like Clara's biscuits and they would give Willie Mae tortillas. There were three other kids who lived down the alley; two boys and a girl. Willie Mae played with them too.

Willie Mae always did love doing hair. She wanted to be a beautician when she was younger, but back then she was afraid. Back then, people said that doing hair, you might get tuberculosis. They said that breathing the fumes would give you respiratory conditions and TB, so that's why she didn't go into it. She would do the hair of all the kids around where we lived. One time this boy going to school with them needed a haircut. Another girl and Willie Mae cut his hair. He had nicks all over.

Coleman was crazy about her. Sometimes Coleman would take Willie Mae with him to Houston when he had to take a truck to pick up or deliver something to Hayden's place there. He'd come home and ask her if she wanted to go. She'd always say, "Yes," and go off with him. If Clara and I weren't at home, Willie Mae would leave us a note. Houston was just fifty-two miles away and was where all our people was. Peggy and Cliff Wilson, our aunt and uncle, and their children lived there. They sure had a slew of kids—twelve of them. Coleman would drop Willie Mae at Peggy and Cliff's where there was always something to do. He did his work and come back for her. That went on until about 1942 or so when the Wilsons moved from Houston to Los Angeles.

We got Willie Mae a dog. Sam was a bull terrier who would sit right there on that porch and watch for her 'til she come from school. He'd know what way she'd come. Sit right there on that porch 'til she come from school. Sam know her from the other kids way down the street. He'd go down the steps and meet her at the gate.

Sometimes one of us would take Sam to the warehouse to pick up the others. Whoever brought the dog out there, that's who he stayed with. If Coleman carried Sam out there, and I ain't carried him out there, he ain't coming back with me. He'd come back with Coleman. That was something. I still ain't figured that out, why he did that. He only came home with the one that brought him.

Money was scarce, but somehow we were always able to have a good time. We usually stayed home in the evenings, never went out nowhere; mighty seldom. Might be on a weekend we'd go to different friends and play cards, you know, like on Sunday, something like that. We'd play card games like Spades and Whist or we'd play dominoes and checkers. We don't play for money, just for fun. We also listened to the radio and the record player. Back then you couldn't listen to a baseball game on radio, but they'd tell you the score.

Galveston had a pretty good little baseball team. I think it was called the "Buccaneers." Didn't have money to go to the ball game. Wasn't that much, but still you had to have it. We did manage to get there though. There were these telephone poles around the stadium and they had a man riding a horse all around the stadium, walking and watching, you know, that no one would climb any of the poles. When he'd go past, we'd run over real fast, climb up that pole and get over the fence and go watch the game.

We also liked to go to the beach. It was a separate beach, but it was nice. Blacks had their own part of the beach with their own bars and ice cream places. We had fun there. The only trouble we had was getting home from the beach. The last bus left the beach at eleven. If you missed the bus, you had to walk home. It was a long ways.

When Willie Mae was about fifteen, she would go to the beach with friends. She supposed to come home by the last bus. One time she miss the bus and come home real late. She say she run all the way, but Clara and I didn't know where she at. I whooped her. Clara didn't like me to do that. Clara wouldn't whoop. She couldn't stand for me to. I didn't whoop too much. Mostly I talk and explain what's right.

Clara always helped, always kept some kind of job to help. Even with me working a lot, things were so tight Clara do maid work for some white folks. Mrs. Kennedy, the woman she worked for, had roomers in her house. Clara cleaned and helped with the cooking and sometimes worked nights when there were parties. We saved enough so that I could buy a truck.

This old man owned Mrs. Kennedy's house and three or four others right in that area. He had told Mrs. Kennedy that if something happened to him to let Clara have the little house in the back. He did pass, but Clara never did get the house. That was fine by me. I didn't want to move there. They already giving parties and different things. She be there late at night sometimes. If she lived in the little house, Mrs. Kennedy could call all hours of the night and work her to death. I know what she gonna do.

I did a lot of different jobs at Hayden. The work was so hard, and the temperature so hot, I stayed real thin. I worked hard to make a living. I was just a man. I had to be a man. I had Clara and Willie Mae to take care of.

One of my regular jobs at Hayden's was to shovel gravel. I loaded and unloaded train cars holding 36 yards of gravel. They paid me $4.00 a car. Each yard of gravel fills a small dump truck. When I shoveled I had to empty the car full of gravel. I did that shoveling by myself for eight hours every day, throwing the gravel over into a bin. I found that I could do much better if I didn't only shovel one way. I'd get in the middle of the car and throw to the right and work for awhile that way. Then I'd change the shovel around and throw to the left and rest my right side. That's just like havin' another man helping me. When you change over to one side, you get relief from the other side. You feel so much better. Thirty-six yards of gravel in that car, unloaded by myself—no problem—just throw it over. Even after eight hours of shoveling, I ain't tired. Ain't no piece of man could unload that carload in eight hours. When I got through and go home, it's just like I never been working. That's just how strong I was back then. I had to be strong to be in the shape I am now, old as I am. If I wasn't in as good shape back then, I would have been dead years ago.

Sometimes I drove a truck delivering small orders, sacks of cement or a little gravel. The boss would bring whatever he wanted delivered to the back of the truck, give it to me and I would take care of the order. Then I'd come back and get back in the rail car and shovel some more gravel.

Another job I had was to load trucks with bricks. Each truck held 1008 bricks, and loading them helped me learn math. Just like with reading, I had to teach myself to count. Each truck held bricks three high, forty-two long and eight wide—1008 bricks. The tongs we used to load and unload with hold 7 bricks. I just learned how to count from them tongs and the rows of bricks. Yeah. If a man order six or seven hundred bricks, I know just how many rows to put on there. It was too many to count one by one. I know the truck that well that after awhile I know just how many to put on by sight. I never made no mistakes. All them years I never forgot how many it hold. That's been a long time.

One time a man wanted 700 bricks, so I carried them there. The guy told Tucker there wasn't 700 bricks there. Tucker went to count them, but he can't count no way. He come back and told me what the man said, and I told him, "I don't need to count again. I know how many bricks there are."

So Tucker went back to count them again. Tucker was going to believe the white man. He ain't going to believe me. He believe what that man say. So Tucker's son went out there to count them. He come back and say, "Yeah Daddy, they're all there." The tongs, they don't lie. They tell me just how many bricks were there—the tongs and the rows.

After I was at Hayden's for awhile, I operated a chair rig, using a crane to move big loads onto a truck. I learned how to operated the chair rig by myself. I used to help the rig operator when he went for his twelve o'clock break. I would cut the steam on the rig for him. Then as soon as he go to eat, I turned the steam back on. I fooled with the rig and learned how to operate it, just like he did. He would never have showed me how to do it. I had to do it on my own. If he'da known that I was fooling with the rig, he'd have died.

One day I was practicing on the rig. Tucker came around and saw the boom moving. He saw what I was doing. When I saw him, I stopped. I come back down there quickly and fooled around down on the ground.

He came over and said, "Get your black behind right on back up that rig." I went back up and Tucker watched me operate the rig with no problem. I could swing the rig around, swoop it down and stop it on a dime, then swing it back up and start again. I could operate the rig just like that white man did. Same thing. I knew everything by watching him. If anything go wrong, I knew how to fix it just like he did. The bossman told me I had a new job and he gave me a little bit more money. They sent the white man to work at Port Arthur, one of the other places Hayden had a business. I stayed working where I was. Everybody came and looked to see a black man operating the rig. I let them know I was just as good as the white operator was.

One of the guys I worked with at Hayden's was Shorty. We were good friends at work. He was the nicest guy you ever want to see. He worked for the warehouse all his life almost. Shorty lived right there in a house at the warehouse. He'd clean up and open the warehouse every morning. He did a lot of jobs there, like somebody came and want a sack of cement or a bucket of sand, that's his job to give it to him. Shorty was a kick.

After I'd been at Hayden's awhile, Shorty came and told me, "Tucker come up and told me that Clarence said that you his brother and Perry his nephew. Tucker want to know where Coleman come in at. I told Tucker that's just an old boy that we picked up."

A few days later I went down to work at the chair rig. Tucker keep following me around. I knowed there was something he wanted to ask me. I stayed out of the way and kept trying to think about what he going ask me.

Finally Tucker come up to me and said, "You changed your damn name, man." I looked at him and laughed. From that day I changed my name back to Johnnie Wilson. It had to be changed anyway because social security numbers were coming out in 1936 and I needed my real name on the card. So Tucker find out just in the right time. My next paycheck was made out to Johnnie Wilson. I used to have my name spelled "Johnny." I didn't like the "y." I liked the "ie" better. I changed it for my social security number.

When my social security card first come out, I put it right on my truck, right there on the visor where I could look at it. In a week's time, I had it in my heart, never forgot it. 452-10-9027. Never forgot it, didn't have to look at nothing, just remember that number. Yeah.

There was a beer brewery near Hayden. I think it was Falstaff. At noon, you'd see all the red Hayden trucks going to the brewery because they give out free beer every day at twelve o'clock. Even though I didn't drink, Coleman and Clarence did. Coleman was always with his bunch of friends. They'd work together and drink together. At noon time, I would always get a bucket too, cause even though I didn't drink, I got beer for the others.

Right across the street from Hayden was a little bar called The Beer Spot. Tucker told us not to go there no more to drink. I don't know why he told us, but he did. The men had a pitcher they used to fill up with beer. Tucker didn't want anyone to take that pitcher over there. Everyone wanted some beer, but nobody wanted to go get it because of what Tucker said. Coleman would always do whatever was wrong. He said, "I'll go get it." They put their little money together to get some beer. Coleman went across the street and got the pitcher full of beer at the bar. Coleman come out and sat down right on the sidewalk and drank that whole pitcher of beer. All he brought back was the foam. Tucker sat right in his window where he could see.

But Tucker didn't do nothing to Coleman. He knowed Coleman was a good worker. He worked with his friend, Benny. They worked together all the time. If they had a car of gravel to unload at a certain place, not at the warehouse but at a job, they go there and unload that carload of gravel in about four hours or something. They worked fast, faster than what a bunch of men could do. They get through about three o'clock in the afternoon. After they finish, they go and drink until their time to go back to the warehouse. Now Tucker, he know all them things, but he didn't bother them because they get the work done.

Benny only weighed about 185 lbs. The truck he used to drive was a big flat bed truck that hauled bricks and things, with them dual back wheels. Sometimes, he'd get half drunk on his back under the truck and pick that side of the truck up with his hands. He was strong. Yeah. I used to tell him, "Benny, you shouldn't do that. That's too much for you." He didn't listen. Him and Coleman liked to drink and have a good time.

Watt was another friend of Coleman's. He was a cement man who lived next door to us. He and his boss didn't work on nothing but sidewalks and runways. Watt was a big drinker. He got broke a lot. How'd he get broke? He gambled at the warehouse. Once Shorty told Watt that Coleman and Benny had crooked dice and that's why Watt kept losing to them.

Watt get mad. He went down to drink, then went home, get his gun and come back fit to kill them. He came into the place and told Coleman, "Come on Coleman. You all come on and walk with this shotgun." He was ready to kill all of them. "Come on let's go." They wouldn't go nowhere. Watt come on closer with the shotgun, and Benny walked over there and took the shotgun out of his hands. He broke the gun down and saw that there were no shells in it. There was a big laugh. People then wasn't like they are now. Now, at least one of them would be dead.

I was in Galveston about four or five years when Levi Compton, a friend from Louisiana, come to Galveston. He came to me and I helped him out. I got him a job and told him to come to my house and Clara would cook for him. For awhile he came and ate with us every day. I got him a job as a chauffeur for Hayden's wife. That's how he got started. If I didn't get him a job, he'd have to go back to Louisiana. He didn't want to do that. Galveston was better than Louisiana.

The Prettiest Thing I Ever Saw

THE WAR BROKE OUT IN 1941 AND YOUNGER MEN WERE GOING OFF TO fight. We were too old to fight. We knew we could make more money at other jobs. Coleman left and went to Seattle to work on dry dock. After Coleman left, my cousin Willie Synoque, Nan's son, come to stay with us. Then George left and went to Los Angeles. After George left, one of Clara's brothers, George Reed came. Our house was always full of family.

In 1941, my brother, George, moved to Los Angeles because his new wife Lydia's brother, Rufus, was there. You had to have some relatives where you gonna to move to. You needed someone. You in bad shape if you don't know nobody cause it was too difficult to settle in without any help. George was working at Quaker Oats and wanted me to come out there. I wasn't too tickled about going there and I wasn't ready to leave Galveston. I did decide to leave my job at Hayden and go to work on the shipyards in Galveston. When I went to get my last check, Mr. Tucker didn't want me to leave. He begged me to stay. But I knew I could make more money working at the shipyard and having enough money to live on was important.

Me and my friend Levi went to work at the dry dock helping finish building ships. Every night I'd call the man I worked with to see if there were jobs in the morning. If there was work, he'd tell us to meet him in the morning. We'd go to a place where we get on the barge that go across the water to the ship we was working on. The man I worked with do little things on the deck like welding. I helped him. He go to work when the ship come in there from Houston, and we finish it up.

When there was work, we had to go at five o'clock in the morning. The trouble was we didn't do nothing until eight o'clock, but we had to be around there. Before eight o'clock you ain't got nothing else to do but sleep. We'd be on the ship, and I'd climb way up and get in a boom and sleep. There was a big place to crawl in and sleep. Once you in there, nobody know you're in there. Way up there, the bossman ain't gonna catch you sleep. Other places you liable to see the bossman at any time. I don't know why we had to be at work at five. I never did figure that out. They must have been making money for us to be there that early. We got paid for being there at five—got paid for sleeping.

After awhile I heard that I could make more money on the waterfront in San Francisco. To work in San Francisco I needed a union book, so I got off the shipyard and got onto the waterfront in Galveston. I needed to work there long enough to get a union book as a longshoreman. Finally in 1944, three years after I started on the shipyards and ten years after I had come to Galveston, I got a union book.

Coleman was already in San Francisco. After he left working dry dock in Galveston, he went to Seattle. Then he left Seattle and come to San Francisco. Coleman was here about a year before I got here. George was gone. Coleman was gone. Only Clara's brother, Clarence, stayed in Galveston. He never left.

My friend, Levi, come out to San Francisco before me. He had an uncle out here so he came out here and found out how things was. He wrote to me right away for to come on out. Levi opened the way and told me when to come.

Same as when I went to Galveston, I came out to San Francisco by myself, leaving Clara and Willie Mae behind. I got the train to come on out here. This time when I traveled, I didn't take a freight train, but rode regular. When I come across the Bay Bridge the city was the prettiest thing I ever saw in my life. I couldn't stop looking at it, just so pretty. I got off the bus at Folsom and Market and caught another bus and went to where Coleman stayed. I came here on September the 22, 1944. I remember that day. The next day, Coleman take me down and got me a job, the next day. Yeah.

When I went to the San Francisco waterfront to get a job, I gave the man my brand new union book. He looked at it. He said, "What are you doing with a new book?"

I thought of a lie right quick. I said, "The other book wore out. That's why I got another one." He looked at me, and had a look on his face that said, "I know he's lying." I know that what he said to hisself. But they needed men so he wrote me up and I got the job. Once I got the job here, I had to work a number of years before I earned a union book again. My experience in Galveston didn't count for nothing with the union out here, but it helped me get the job.

As a longshoreman, I loaded and unloaded ships. It wasn't like it was in the southern states, the white on one end of the ship and the colored on the other end. In San Francisco the crews were mixed white and black men. Work with all kinds of people on the ships. I even learned how to write Chinese. It's not easy to learn how to write Chinese. It's not too hard either. I used to write it just like the Chinese. Now how I learned how to write it ... At the top of the hall, there was a sign that said, "No Smoking," with American on top and Chinese under it. In a week's time, I learned how to write "No Smoking" in Chinese. I learned how to write it without looking at it.

One day a ship come in there with some Chinese men on there. I wrote "No Smoking" on some paper and held it where they could see it. In little or no time, more men were running out of their hall there, fifteen or twenty Chinese men, looking at me writing it. They just about had a fit. They look at me and look at me. They wondered how did I learn it. I wrote it again. They didn't know what to do. They never knew how I learned to write just like they do. They couldn't understand. They never saw no black man writing Chinese before.

They bring the load in and carry it in and out of the hold with winches. In the hold you took the loads and put it on hand pulled trucks and pulled the trucks where you were going to stack them. You stack it up about four feet high and go right on stacking, making a runway wide enough for the truck to go through to pick up the boxes on the other end. Working in the hold was tough work. After a few years, they put jitneys down in the hold to pull the loads. You didn't have to pull the load by hand. The jitney bring the load right where you unload it. That made it much better. Yeah.

Generally you had to "plug in" each time you finished a job. Plugging in meant that every time you get through with a ship, you gotta go "plug in"—kind of check in—for another job. If you were on a plug, you never had to go to the hall unless you wanted to. Some guys were so greedy, they stayed on the plug.

If you could get on a work gang, you didn't have to plug in. Gangs had about twelve people on them. At night you'd call the hall and they tell you if there was work the next day. If the gang was working they tell you just where to go to. Sometimes he'd say, "Come down, there's plenty of gravy." That meant there was plenty of work and I could go down the next day and work. If there was no work, they tell you to call back tomorrow night. I'd work during the day, then call the hall at night.

The gangs worked everywhere, no certain place. Sometimes you worked in San Francisco, or you might be dispatched to Oakland, Redwood City or Vallejo, everywhere. They had buses to take us where we needed to go work.

We worked with partners in the hold. It was important to have a partner that worked hard. It don't work to have one partner studying and fooling around or taking stuff home while you work, make me do all his work while he playing. Some people do you just like that. You be surprised how guys do you. They do any little thing to throw you off from what you supposed to do. Most of my partners was okay. Most of the men work hard, but some take advantage of you.

I work with a man for a couple of days and find out just what kind of guy he is. If he gonna make me do all the work while he doing nothing, finally you get tired of that. I say, "Fine, I don't want to work with you anymore. I get somebody else." Some kind of way, I get rid of them. It wasn't always too easy to change partners. I got to look around to see somebody to work with that had somebody he didn't want to work with. Then we work things out. Sometimes it took time to fit it all together.

I'm a person that can't work with a guy that always squabbles, cause I ain't gonna give him something to squabble about. If one of my partners was hard to get along with, always cussing and something ain't right, after a time it'd make me angry with him. You try real hard to get along, but if you can't you move on. You don't let people keep beating on you. I'm gonna quit that guy and get me another partner, somebody that I ain't got to holler with. It don't make no sense with two working partners who have to be always squabbling. It don't make no sense because I don't like to squabble. It makes your day easier when you ain't got to be always squabbling.

I knew two guys good, one guy and his partner always fighting one another. They worked together. They drank together. They squabbled together. One day one killed the other. It supposed to be an accident, but it came out of squabbling. That don't make no sense to me. You mean to tell me I'm supposed to live like that? No way I can live like that, fighting and arguing and cussing at each other.

One time my partner was a guy named Peachie. Most of the time Peachie was as nice a guy as can be. Most of the time I like working with him. But on Monday mornings he come in drunk. While I'm trying to work, he be pulling on me, all around, talking in my face. I just got tired of it. So, the next couple of Mondays, he come down the hall, I said, "I ain't gonna work with you." I told him I get another guy who work with me; he get another guy to work with him. Every Monday morning he come in drunk, I find someone else to work with. He wanted to work with me, so he quit getting drunk on Monday mornings. I took him back as a partner. It come out all right.

I was here about three weeks when Levi decided not to stay. At that time it was hard out here. There just wasn't enough housing—you just couldn't find no place to stay, there were so many people. He had a large family. He had seven kids. When he found out what it takes to take care of them out here, he thought he could take better care of his family back in Galveston.

When Levi went back to Galveston, he went back to work on the waterfront. After a year, he come to be a walking boss and made good money there. If Levi had stayed out here, he would have been a walking boss here too, but it would have taken a long time. They didn't start hiring new walking bosses for five or six years after I was here.

If I'd a went to fifth grade, I could easy make a walking boss cause I know the business, know how to take care of it. They want to make me a walking boss, but like, somebody get hurt, I wouldn't know what paper work to do. Ain't nobody to teach me what to do. They wanted me to be a walking boss, but I said, "no." My reading and writing wasn't that good. If Levi had stayed out here, I'd a been a walking boss on the waterfront, cause he'd a taught me just what to do.

I stayed in the hold for a long time. In the late 50's, I come to find out I'm the oldest man in the hold. Working in the hold of a ship, loading and unloading all day, was tough work. I was more than fifty years old and I wanted to get out of the hold. You had to learn some kind of way to get out of the hold and get you another job so you wouldn't have to work so hard.

First thing I tried, I started driving winches in the same gang I worked. The boss told me, he say, "You ain't gonna like that," but I figured I'd like it like the rest of it. I always find a way to like what I did. Not this time. Sure enough I didn't like it. There was too much exposure. Winch drivers are out on the pier in the cold all the time, just standing there working the levers, carrying the load up and down from the bottom of the hold to the top of the ship and back again. It didn't matter how many coats you had on, the air went right through you. The money didn't mean that much to me for me to stay there and misuse my life on account of the money. My health was too important to me. I quit that and went back in the hold.

When I was working the winches, there was this white boy who worked down in the hold of the ship. He was there when I got in that gang. He wanted to learn so bad, and I tried to teach him. I just could not learn him. He could not learn it. You could stand up or sit down to work the levers. He stand up and put his hands on the levers. I get behind him and put my hands on top of his hands. I still couldn't learn him how to drive winches. I was making him do it, using his hands, under mine; making him do it, carrying a load out, and putting them in. My hands on top of his hands, I just never could learn him. So he got disgusted and he quit trying.

Later he got to be a walking boss. What he did, he fired a gang the first night he started as walking boss. No good reason. That next morning, they had his papers right there, waiting. They fired him right there. You just can't do that. How many hundred thousand dollars they lost that night just by him firing the gang. Just cause he a walking boss he fired a gang. That's the worst thing he could have done.

There was another guy I knew who was so good at what he did they made him a gang boss. He couldn't handle it. He work hisself to death and the men, too. He tell them to do something. They don't jump up and do it, he'd jump down there and do it hisself. You need to teach the guys if they don't know. Just take time and teach them. They'll listen. He don't have that kind of patience. No, no. He didn't have sense enough to use his men like his boss used him. He didn't have that kind of knowledge. They took the gang from him. You got to know how to work with people you over.

These guys didn't have what Tom Porter, my baseball manager in Louisiana, had. Tom was a good guy. Tom knows how to handle men, knows how to talk to them. If you the boss and you gonna fuss at me, I can't say nothing back to you. You can't go to them and talk to them like you talk to somebody walking down the street or something. Tom was that kind of guy. He knows just how to handle men real good.

I was still thinking how to get out of the hold. Working the winches wasn't right, but there were two dock men whose job it was to hook the load onto the winches. Their jobs were on the dock, doing nothing except hooking the loads on. You hook the load on, sit down, wait until they unload it, unhook it, sit down again. They ain't doing nothing, just sitting there. That's all they did. They had a shed to go into when the weather was bad, or just to sit down inside. I decided to stay in the hold until I could get one of their jobs. I knew one of them was going to retire pretty soon. He did.

It wasn't too long after I stopped driving the winches that I finally got the job on the dock—about fourteen years after I'd started working on the waterfront. When the loads come down, me and my partner just stand there, hook them loads on, get 'em back on the ship. We sit there and wait 'til we get ready for the next load. I sit down, hook the load on, sit down, wait until they unload it, unhook it, sit down again. I ain't doing nothing, just sitting there. That's all I did, and while I was sitting and waiting for another load to hook, I'd fish. I brought home some beautiful fish. I had this job for about ten years. I remember that in the winter, they put a tent up. We'd take the box that the tent had been in and set it up in the doorway of the shack. We'd cover it and make a seat just big enough for me and my partner sit on. It made the shack as comfortable as sitting in my house. We enjoyed that. That was nothing but fun for me.

Our job was easy, but you had to be careful with anything you do on the waterfront. You couldn't ever wear long gloves when you worked hooking the loads. One time before I had the job, a guy got his long glove caught in where the hook attached to the load. The man operating the lift set the lifter to raise the load. He must have gone back to look at something else, look at a ship or something, and didn't pay no attention to the load. When the hooked load was picked up, the man with the glove went along with it. There was no way for him to get loose with all that weight on the load. The guy was up there with it and no one saw him. When the load was set down the man broke loose, dropped down and died right there.

I had the same partner almost the whole time I worked hooking loads. He retired before I did. Fritz was a good partner in one way. The one nice thing about him, me and him would go fishing. He liked to fish. I liked to fish. He'd catch fish and give them to me. If he got a big one, he take that and fillet it and give them to me.

In another way he wasn't a good partner, on account of he was all for hisself. I would always have to be the one to yield to him. He would never do for me. If we got a ship coming in, we got to drive down to Pier 41 to catch the boat to go out to the ship that was going to land somewhere else. I would drive him down there. He never would drive me. He's the kind of guy that wouldn't help you no kinda way.

It was the same with union dues. If I go pay my union dues, I pay his dues, too. I'd always ask him before he go on vacation, did he want me to pay his dues. One time I went on vacation and he never said nothing to me about dues. When I come back, I find out my dues ain't paid. We both met down there at the hall where I paid the dues. That's the type of guy he was. Long as you're helping him, it's okay.

I'm Easy Too

WHEN I FIRST MOVED TO SAN FRANCISCO, LEVI AND I STAYED WITH Coleman for a few days, then we stayed with another friend that moved from Galveston. There were so many people who moved here then. If you were lucky, you might find a little hole somewhere, a room somewhere with a community kitchen. But it was hard to find a place to stay unless you know somebody. There wasn't much building going on, so you just had to wait until you could find something. After Levi left, I finally found a room in a big hotel right there by the Ferry Building on Sacramento Street near Market. A friend of mine was living there, and he got me a place.

I only weighed 167 lbs. when I moved to San Francisco. Back in Galveston, it's hot. Between the heat and the hard work I didn't weigh much. And when I came to San Francisco, I liked to starve to death because I didn't know how to cook. I was eating in cafés and got so I couldn't stand the smell. So I had to learn to cook myself.

My brother, Coleman, he's a good cook. He do the cooking for his friends and have little parties and different things. He loved to cook and have people over. Viola, his wife, didn't like to be with people, but he sure did. He learned how to cook when he was young, when he was on his own. Me and Coleman lived a good ways apart, but close enough. I went to Coleman all the time so he could teach me. I never learned nothing about how to cook until he taught me.

In the hotel where I stayed, there was a kitchen down the hall. I didn't use it. I learned how to cook on the gas room heater. You put gas in the heater, light it and it warmed the room real nice. That heater makes enough fire just for you to cook a nice meal. I cook rice, steaks, anything I want. Then I made it all right until Clara got out here. Clara was a good cook, my wife. She was a good cook! Cook some of everything. I ain't never saw nothing she don't know how to cook. She was raised up in the country and a big family. Her mother was a good cook. That's why she's a good cook.

After about a year, Clara joined me. When Clara came, I learned how to cook even more from her. I just watched her and learned how to cook—gumbo, cakes, sweet potato pie—anything I want to cook, I can cook it. I still love to cook. When Clara came, she brought our granddaughter Betty with her. Willie Mae stayed back in Texas with her husband.

Willie Mae married Leon Holoman a little before I got my union book in Galveston. Willie Mae met Leon at her girlfriend, Leanna Charles' house about a block from where we lived. Leon lived next door to Leanna. After awhile, he'd come by our house and she started seeing him. She was only sixteen. Leon was twenty-one. He was a man. She was too young. Clara and I weren't happy about her doing that and not finishing school. She was too young to get married and have a baby. After they married, Willie Mae and Leon lived in a little apartment across the street from us.

Willie Mae couldn't keep Betty cause she had to work and there was no one to take care of her. I think I started calling Betty "Cat" about then. I don't know why I give her that name. I guess it's because she cried so much. Willie Mae thinks she cried so much because we spoiled her.

Clara didn't like it in San Francisco. It was a strange place for her. It didn't seem like home. Living in a residence hotel made it hard. She only stayed a couple months and went back to Galveston. She lived with Willie Mae while Leon was in the service.

I didn't want her to go. I told her I wasn't going back. I told her, "You go back, I'm staying here. I got a good job. I'm not going back. Now you wanna go, you go, but I'm not going." I sure miss her when she went. It was tough for me when she went back, but I wanted to stay.

When Clara got back to Galveston, things didn't work out like she thought it was gonna work out. When she left, she thought I was gonna go with her. She was back in Galveston for almost one year. She found out I wasn't coming, so she wrote me to send her some money. She come back and brought Betty with her again. When she come back, she made herself at home.

Clara always kept a job to help. Her working sure helped. That's how we got started here. She got a job at the Buchanan St. YMCA. She made beds and cleaned rooms, and so forth. Clara helped me all of the time we were together. She would always work. Clara wasn't like some other women who never want to work. She was happy that she had a job and worked every day, just like me.

After Clara come back out here, we kept on asking Willie Mae to come on out. She got lonesome for us too and joined us after about a year, in '47, bringing her baby son, Sonny, along with her. Sonny's real name was Leon after his father, but they called him Sonny after an uncle. When I went to get her at the Ferry Building, Willie Mae was crying. She started me to cry, I was just so glad to see her. I hadn't seen her in about three years. Willie Mae and the children lived with us in our hotel. She had a room down the hall from us. We wanted to find another place to live, but there wasn't enough places.

At Army and Third, right on the corner, there were seventy-five or eighty trailers. Coleman and Viola lived there for awhile. Then he got an apartment nearby when some friends of his told him about a vacant apartment and vouched for him with the landlord. After he found the apartment, he let us have his trailer. We moved there until I could find another place. It gave us more room and privacy than at the hotel. At each end of the trailer was a little couch, with the kitchen in the middle. We slept on one end and Willie Mae and the kids slept on the other.

Willie Mae decided to stay in San Francisco, but first she took Sonny and Betty back to Texas where Leon was to get her stuff. Leon wasn't sure he wanted to move out here, but she had decided to come anyway. She was in Galveston for six or seven months before she came back.

Before Willie Mae got back, I found a place to live on O'Farrell, behind Girl's High School. The white lady who owned the building come there and said, "This is my house and you all have to leave." I thought I had a lease for a flat in a building, but I didn't. I found out that the colored real estate woman I dealt with was a crook. We give the rent money to the real estate woman. She take the money but she didn't give it to the landlord. It was the same for the all the people in the building. The white lady let us stay for a while, but we had to pay more rent. I had no where to go. It took time to find some place else.

We wanted a place we could buy. In 1947, I think, I found a place on Webster with two flats, #509, between Hayes and Fell that I wanted to buy. There was a downstairs that had a living room, a bedroom, a kitchen and a small room in the back. The upstairs had a small room in the front, a living room, a kitchen, a dining room and a bedroom. It was just a nice size.

I needed three hundred more dollars to close the deal. Even though Clara worked and helped with money, we didn't have enough for the down payment. I wasn't in San Francisco long enough for to borrow no money from a bank. I tried to borrow from people I knew, but couldn't borrow nothing. Now, what I'm gonna do? So I studied and studied. Where I'm gonna get the $300?

So I go to play the "Chinaman"—something like a lottery and win $336.00. Just like that! Three hundred and thirty six dollars. You couldn't never be no luckier than that. I rented out the top flat and we lived in the lower. That's the only time I tried something like that lottery. It sure helped.

For a long time we didn't have no TV. Sometimes in the evening, Clara and I would listen to the radio. There was a great preacher, Carl Anderson, in Oakland who we liked to listen to. He came on every night at nine o'clock. Reverend Anderson could sing good. One night when we listening to Reverend Anderson, Coleman came through the door. He heard the singing. He took his fist and broke the screen on my radio. The radio never stopped playing. That music sounded so good, he didn't know nothing else to do but take his fist and break the screen. I guess he didn't want to hear church music.

Coleman was half drunk that night. He cut his hand and then fell out on the floor after he hit the radio. I didn't say nothing. I never said nothing. My wife spread a blanket over him. When he got sober, he got up and went on home. So after that, he never did it no more. He thought I was going to be pulling on him, trying to get him in the bed. We left him laying there. That learned him. That taught him something. He didn't do it no more, at least not by us.

When Coleman was sober, he was just as good as anybody else. He didn't drink too much. But sometimes he'd be so drunk, he had to almost crawl up the steps, but he never had no accident. No matter how drunk he'd get, he'd know where he's going and ain't gonna run into nothing. Never hit nobody. Yeah, yeah. I don't know how he did it. Nobody else know how he did it. I guess he knew when to stop and he knew when to leave. He was lucky.

Willie Mae moved back out here and stayed with us there until Leon came. This time when she came, she brought my brother, Monk, with her. Leon was a veteran, so they moved into an apartment at Crocker Amazon where there were army apartments.

Monk stayed here for awhile, then went to Los Angeles and stayed with George. My nephew Perry came out here too. He left Texas 'fore I did. Went to Los Angeles first. Then he went in the army. After he got out of the army, he come stay with me awhile here. He's been around here ever since. A lot of our family came out to California.

When Willie Mae first went to work out here, she worked at a medical lab out on Mission. She started to do bookkeeping out there. It was a good little job, but they just started this clinic, and there wasn't much money. She needed a job that paid better, so she went to work at the Y with Clara. The Y had a rule that members of the same family couldn't work at the same Y, but her last name was different, so it worked out okay. They rode to work together every day.

When Clara worked at the Y and young servicemen would come in, away from home, she'd bring them home and feed them. Clara was a just a nice person. She'd help anybody. She'd be bringing people home all the time. We'd say "Clara, you don't know these people," and she'd say, "They're fine, they're fine." On Christmas she'd get stuff for people that didn't have. The Y would give baskets for people at Christmas, Thanksgiving and Easter and she'd put in the names of people who needed help. She was always doing something to help people.

Clara was like her own mother. Lutishie Reed was a fine person, her mother, a fine woman. Lutishie was joyful with everybody. She's the kind of woman if somebody didn't have nowhere to stay, she'd take him in 'til he get someplace to stay. If somebody passed, she would take people's kids. That's just the kind of woman she was. Everybody liked her.

Soon after I came to in California, I played baseball again. I just see men playing ball on 7th Street. I just go out there and talk with them, get used to 'em. That's how I started playing with them. We played every weekend near 7th Street and 5th Street meet, Seals Stadium, where you go on the freeway now. There wasn't nothing there, nothing, just lots where you play ball. Then no houses, nothing, just where you play ball. I was the pitcher. We had a nice little club, the Western Sugar Baseball Team. I played with them about two and a half years until they start building freeways there.

Before I came to San Francisco, I didn't vote. When I got here, I wanted to vote. I forgot to get everything straight before I go down there to the courthouse for to register to vote. I didn't know whether I was a Democrat or a Republican. When I went there and they asked me, I just couldn't tell him. I was upset, and said, "Well, I'll have to come back." I had to come back and get it straight whether I'm a Democrat or a Republican. Ever since then I be voting every election. It's important to vote. Lots of people never vote. They think it's something crazy or something. But I know it's important. Couldn't vote in Louisiana.

In 1946 I taken asthma. I taken it bad. I never had it before I come to San Francisco. I went to different doctors at Kaiser. The doctors didn't do me no good. I don't know why. They just didn't seem to do me no good. My breathing was so bad 'til at night Clara would be laying out asleep and I'm sitting in the chair aside the bed. I couldn't lay down. I couldn't sleep. It would make it worse. I'd get right up out of the chair in the morning, go fix my breakfast, give Clara coffee and go on to work. I ain't never slept, just sit in the chair.

It just got so bad that when I was at work I had to be the last one out of the hold, cause I had to stop between decks and rest before I could come out of the hold. The hold is like a three-story building and it took me a long time to get out of it. Going up and down the ladder was tough even if you didn't have asthma. What you put your feet on is just about as big as two fingers wide. All your weight is just on that skinny rung. That makes it bad walking up and down.

One particular day I went down the hold in the morning. They was unloading, uncovering hatches and it made all that dust. I just had asthma so bad. I couldn't breath. I had to stop working. I went over there in the corner. I kneeled on one knee and I talked to Jesus Christ. I talked to him. I prayed to him right there. I got religion right there in the hold of that ship. I stayed there on my knees, and I comes to feeling better and better. I stood up. I went on back there and went to work. I was feeling so good and so happy. I didn't feel anything bad no more. At two o'clock, I went on right out of the hold with the rest of the men, breathing all right. Just so happy.

I come on back to the house and told Clara, "Sunday, I'm going with you to church." Clara was very happy that I had found religion. Church was very important to her. You ain't gonna keep her out of church. She's gonna go to Macedonia Church on Sutter Street. Clara was an usher there and always tried to get me to go with her. I'd go sometimes, but not too much before I got religion. Before I got religion, I never go to church unless I go with somebody because if I go by myself everybody be looking at me walking in and I get shamed.

The next day I just happened to be off. Clara was going to work. I had to talk to somebody that was a Christian that I could talk to that wanted to talk to me like I wanted to talk to them about Jesus Christ. Coleman's wife, Viola, was in San Francisco General. She was the one I wanted to talk to. I went to visit her. I sat there and talked to her two or three hours. I told her, I say, "I gotta get baptized Sunday."

But I was feeling so good and so happy, I couldn't wait 'til Sunday. I wanted to be baptized now. I told Clara, "I got to go get baptized. I just can't stay out of the water. I know I got religion."

At that time Billy Graham was right here at Glad Tidings Church, a big church on Eddy and Webster. I went right over there to that church and I walked in. I never stopped. I walked straight 'til I got up to the pulpit and shook his hand. I told him I want to get baptized tonight. And, he baptized me that night, that same night. That's a wonderful man. Just listening to him talk, if he don't change your mind, ain't nobody gonna change you. I just sat there and listened to him with joy.

On Sunday I went to Macedonia with Clara. Reverend Osmond baptized me again. He didn't recognize the Glad Tidings baptism. I didn't care how many times I got baptized. It didn't bother me. I had religion. I had religion. I know.

I started going to circle meetings with Clara and really like them. Circle meetings were once a week at different people's houses. The church mapped out where you going to on which days. There was always about seven or eight people at a meeting, just enough for a group. At meetings you read from the Bible and talk about what you read. They teach the Bible. You learn so much just by going to circle meetings.

Religion is still in my heart. I still got religion. I know I've been converted. Can't nobody tell me nothing to keep me from going to church, cause I know I've been converted. I still goes to Macedonia. I ain't gonna quit my church. Me and my wife been there ever since we been in California. Even when some of the church members left to follow a preacher who started another church, I stayed right there. Nobody can't move me from Macedonia. Must be about four or five different preachers since I've been there. I'll stay there as long as I live. As long as I live, I'll be right there at that church. Yeah.

Clara and I always got along, but Willie Mae had a tough time. She married when she was sixteen, but she came to find out that her husband wasn't nothing. He was an alcoholic and wasn't able to stop drinking. Leon had been in the service and after the war got a good government job. But he didn't want to work, so he did something to make them fire him. He was a good mechanic too; good at working on cars. Could'a done that, but too much drinking. They were fussing and squabbling all the time. He want to misuse her and fight the kids. I keep on her 'til she finally quit him and got a divorce.

After she quit him, he told me he didn't have nothing else to live for. Just throwed himself away. I wrote his daddy to come out here and get him. He did and carried him back to Galveston. Leon got pretty good back there. He working at the filling station. But later on, something happened to his foot and he got some oil or something on it. His foot swole up and they take him to the hospital. Finally the foot mollified or something. It killed him. That's how he died.

After she quit Leon, Willie Mae moved back in with us on Webster. At first she lived with us in our apartment, but when Jean, the woman who lived upstairs, moved, Willie Mae moved up there with the children. We had to help her out. Things was tough at that time. I couldn't help her like I wanted, but we did what we could. Yeah.

After about ten years on Webster, we decided to find another place. I worked with a real estate man who helped. We bought a set of flats on Belvedere off of 17th—#577-579. The house was bigger than Webster. Downstairs had two bedrooms, a living room and a dining room. The kitchen was kinda small, but we had the dining room which made it nice. Upstairs was the same. We stayed there for a long time.

In 1958 or 9, Willie Mae married again. My son-in-law, Jack, had a barbershop right downtown near Third Street, three blocks from Market. He had a nice barbershop with three chairs. Sometimes he would drive a cab. They were doing okay.

About this time, I borrowed a couple a hundred dollars from Morris Plan. Jack's shop was a couple of blocks from the guy I borrowed the money from. So I gave Jack the money to pay back on my loan. One day the guy I owed the money to told me the bill ain't been paid. I go to see Jack and asked him why he didn't pay it. He didn't say nothing.

Then I come to find out from Jack's best friend that Jack run back and forth to the horse race in my brand new car. He's spending my money, running women, running to the race track in my brand new car. I told my daughter something got to be done to stop him. He ain't gonna drive my car no more, not to go to no racetrack and run with women. He do me like that, he'll do something else.

Willie Mae decided to quit Jack. After she left him, they put Jack in jail 'cause he wasn't paying for his children he had before he married Willie Mae. Come to find out he had children and wives Willie Mae didn't know nothing about. They locked him up for two or three years. When he gets out, he come back to Willie Mae at work and talk to her. He talk to her and she talk to him. He come back to the house to talk to Clara. Clara was easy. She wanted Willie Mae to go back to him. Willie Mae would not do it. No, she's through with him. Wouldn't have nothing to do with him. He went crazy. He just knew she gonna take him back. He just know he's gonna get her back, and do her like he did before. But it just didn't happen. He called her on her job and she wouldn't even talk to him. He come to the house and she wouldn't talk to him. Willie Mae just didn't want nothing to do with him. He call, but she hung the phone up.

Willie Mae always went to church like my wife did. In the 1960's, after she quit Jack, she met Ivery Mackey at church. Once she met Mack, Willie Mae became more involved in church. She started ushering in church. Mack was pretty nice and they got married in 1963. After she got married, Willie Mae went to school all over again with Mack and they both got their high school degrees. They've been married for more than thirty years now. This time she got a good husband. Mack got a good job. He worked as a cement finisher. Willie Mae helped raise Mack's son, Benny.

Around the same time, Betty got married to Lorrel Anderson. After a couple of years he got sick and Betty liked to lose him. He had a burst appendix. After they operated on him, he couldn't work. My wife easy. I'm easy too. Cat brought him to the house. One day I got off work and come on home. There he was in the bed, sick. He stayed there for a year 'til he got well and got on his feet. That was a long time to be sick. Cat, she had to see after him, the wounds and things, take care of them. And it hurt her so bad just to see him like that. You don't figure he'da been living, the way he was cut up. By being a young man, he pulled through. Thank the Lord. The Lord brought him through.

In 1966 my cousin, Phillip Wilson, moved in with us after he and his wife fell out in Los Angeles. He just didn't want to stay down there, so he come up here to live with us. It seemed like we always had someone with us. For awhile he worked as a longshoreman, but he had to stop because he had a heart condition.

A few years after Phillip moved in with us, my neck started getting all swollen. I was going to Kaiser[xiv] in San Francisco and they worked on it and sent me to Kaiser in Oakland. They kept me there on the table for about two hours while they examined me. They sent me back to San Francisco. It was still swollen. They never told me to come in or nothing, but I went back in to see what they were going to do. They examined me and they didn't do nothing. They said to come back. When I went back again, they give me some stuff to make it go away.

For a little while, the swelling went away about the size of my finger, then stopped and laid there for about five or six months. Then it started growing again. I had to go back out to Kaiser, but they wasn't doing nothing. In 1971 Willie Mae carried me to U.C. San Francisco Medical Center and they examined me for about three weeks. They told me there wasn't nothing else to do but take my thyroid out. It had gotten so bad by being there so long, they had to take out one of my vocal cords. That's why my voice sounds the way it does.

Slowing Down Some

IN 1965 WHEN I WAS SIXTY-FIVE, I RETIRED FROM THE WATERFRONT. NOW that I'm ninety-five, I've been retired longer than I worked there. I worked for twenty-five years and I have been retired for twenty-nine years. The waterfront don't owe me nothing no more. They've been paying retirement for a long time. Clara retired from her job at the YMCA in 1969. She worked there for twenty-three years.

Clara had high blood pressure, but she was okay. After she retired we discovered that she had sugar. That really upset her. But she was doing just fine. Then her knee swelled up. We thought it was arthritis. She didn't like to go to the doctor and she didn't tell me when she'd be sick. She never would say nothing. I don't know why, but she wouldn't tell me. Probably didn't want to worry me. Clara didn't want to worry anybody. She was okay until 1972. Then she had a massive heart attack and stroke and passed away.

We were married 47 years when she passed. I liked to passed away too. When Clara died, I like to have fell apart. I just couldn't do nothing without her. She was my backbone. Just be there. That's all she had to do. And she wasn't there. Just drove me crazy, insane. I just couldn't get over it. Clara was always on my mind. Couldn't get her off of my mind. Day in and day out, she was on my mind, don't care where I go.

After she passed away, that just got me confused. I was doing things that I never did before. I wasn't taking care of business, just doing any little thing that I wasn't supposed to do; running around with girls, anything to have a good time with somebody that could get her off of my mind. Make me relax a little.

I even slowed up going to church. Then I just quit going all together. Members of my church come and talk to me, but it didn't do nothing. About two or three months after I quit going to church, I take a little bit of asthma back. I didn't have asthma for more than twenty years. That just shows how Jesus Christ work. He put asthma back on me just a little bit—

just to let me know that I was doing wrong. That was a blessing. The way that He treated me was just like somebody talking to me. I put on my suit and I flew to that church. I couldn't get to that church fast enough. I started going back to church and taking care of business better. Ever since then, I keep going to church. Now I only get a little asthma in December or January, then no more 'til the next year.

My cousin, Phillip, was still living with me at the time Clara passed. That helped me some. Then he passed in 1975, three years after Clara died. I didn't want to stay in the house no more, so I sold it. The house on Belvedere was paid for. I paid over $7,000 and paid it off. No problem there. Before Clara passed, I thought about borrowing $10,000 on the house and buying another one with two flats to rent. I was going to buy it and turn it over a real estate company, let them take care of it. That way, I'd never have trouble getting people in and out. They gonna get 'em out if they got to. That's what I was gonna do. Then I would have had some regular income coming. I would have been worth something, but then Clara pass away, and I didn't do it.

I had to move away. I could have stayed there. I wasn't afraid or nothing. I do all right 'til night come. When night come, I just couldn't sit there and look at TV. I don't know, it just drive me crazy. I had to do something.

I sold the house, and I give Betty some money for a down payment on a larger house on Crusader and went to stay with her. That started them out and gave me another place to live. Looking back, I shouldn't have sold the house on Belvedere. It would have been nice to have. It would be worth some money now.

It took me thirteen years before I got any kind of relief from Clara's death. Me and her were so close together. It was tough. I kind of wore it off and come to myself. It still took me a long time to get over Clara. Thirteen years, that's a long time. I finally got relief that I could live without her.

Part of what made me get relief from her death was doing some of the things I'd thought about doing after I retired. When I retired, I knew I can't stop doing things. I know a lot of guys who only live two weeks or three weeks or maybe a couple of months after they stop work. After retiring, they go. They throw themselves at work, then they got nothing to do.

They just sit around and look at TV and it gets so they can't go nowhere. I be doing the same thing if I just sit here and look at TV, never get out of the house when I retired. I'd soon be so I couldn't walk. I knew I gotta keep moving so I thought of what I could do with my time. I thought about making different things with wood. I thought of that. And I thought about helping my friend Taylor fix cars.

Taylor was a good friend of mine, and a good mechanic. I get up just like I was going to work and go help him, just to get away from the house. He sure helped me out a whole lot. Just to have somewhere to go and to be with him and see how he work and help him. That helped to get my mind straighten out. If I wouldn't had that to do and my wood work, I don't know what would have come of me, cause my mind wasn't just right, wasn't just exactly right. You hear the saying with one gone, it don't be too long before the other be gone. If something like working with Taylor don't come up and I didn't start going around him, get my mind offa her, I guess I'd been gone too. That's a great help to me.

Then, after I moved in with Betty, I started doing a little work with wood in the garage doing different things. I'd sit and think and carve. That helped my mind, building things with wood. And people passing by, they stop and see what I'm doing. That helped me out a whole lot. So did Sam, a dog Betty brought to the house. Got him out of the garbage can somewhere. He grew to be about a foot high. He was a cute dog. We called him "Sam," just like the dog we had in Galveston.

I took Sam and trained him to bring me things. I trained him to bring my slippers. I carry them in the living room and put them down. He wouldn't pay them no mind. So I kept doing it and finally he start to pick them up. Then I leave the slippers in the living room and come back to the bed with him and tell him to go get 'em. He go in the living room, come right back, jump up on the bed with a slipper in his mouth. I take it from him, "Now go get the other one." He go get the other one. Train him just like that. I would put a piece of a treat, when he wasn't watching me, somewhere where he couldn't see it. And I'd say, "Look around. Look around." He'd start to looking, finally he see it. He go there and get it and eat it. I had him trained good.

Sam liked to be with me. When I worked in the garage, Sam liked to run in the street near me. The garage door stayed open all the time cause I was always doing something there. Sometime when I'm going upstairs I'd call him, make him stay in the garage, and sometime I let him stay out. He run around out there, never go nowhere, just run around there near the house. One day I went upstairs and left him outside. When I come back down, he was gone. I think somebody stole him, cause he wouldn't go off by himself. I know he wouldn't. No. No.

In '76 or '77, Willie Mae and Mack bought some land up in Clearlake. There wasn't anything on it then, just a field. They been up there looking around. Mack saw an ad that the Hayman Corporation would be selling some property at Clearlake at the Airport Hilton. They went to the Hilton and bought some property. They wanta go see it, but the man told them that the roads need fixing, so they didn't go. After the rains, they went up to see the property. The land they bought was way back in the boonies.

Mack didn't like where the lot was. He told them that he wanted something he could use in his lifetime, not something to leave for his kids. The man show them some more land and took them where they are now. The man told them they could have this other property for more money. He didn't think Mack had the money. When Mack start to write him a check the man said, "I'll have to see what my boss is going to say. I don't know if he'll let it go for that amount."

They went to the office where the boss was. They talked and talked and talked and finally Mack got about an acre and a half. Later they bought more. Altogether they didn't spend $3,000. The property was owned by old Italians who said that no blacks or dark color could buy the property. After they died out, their kids didn't care.

Mack and Willie Mae got themselves a mobile home. The mobile was sitting by itself on the land. There was nothing close by until others bought in. It had two little bedrooms and a living room. Hayman said the sewer would be through the same year, but it took four years to get the sewer. Later on they got a modular home with three bedrooms. They still got the land.

We love to go up to the Lake. We have peaches, grapes, walnuts and figs. When the fruit is in season, Willie Mae makes fine jam. We play games and cards at the lake with different friends. We still play spades and whist and dominoes and checkers. No money, just fun.

In 1984 or so, I was driving along on the street. All of a sudden as I drove across Fillmore, I blacked out about ten feet before Webster. The wheel stayed straight as I passed Webster and I went on for about ten feet before I come to. I stopped right there and looked back and say to myself, 'Supposing a car had been coming. Supposing I'da been on the Bay Bridge or anywhere with a lot of cars. I mighta been killed.' Just happened there were no cars there. That telling me something right there. Right then I drove that truck to Sonny's house and put it in the garage. I went right on and put that truck up and never drove it since. I shoulda went to the hospital, but I didn't. I didn't go to a doctor either. I just went home. It was hard to give up driving. I used to drive everywhere. It hurt me, but I thought about it would save my life if I don't drive, so I just didn't worry about it. I took the bus where I want to go.

I was sitting right at the kitchen table cooking sweet potato pie when I had another heart attack at Betty's in 1986. This time, I went to the hospital. I had them laughing at the hospital. They couldn't believe that at my age I was cooking sweet potato pie.

I was in the hospital about a week. They told me that my heart came out of the socket. They had a machine that put it back. They did one jerk, got it back in place. I never could figure that out. How could I have a heart attack and the heart come out of its socket? And guys, playing football, getting hit; nothing ever happen to them like that.

At about the same time I had my second heart attack, Mack had a stroke. When he first came home from the hospital, he couldn't walk or talk. He still don't have the use of one of his hands. Willie Mae stopped work to take care of him. She told me to come stay with her and Mack. She was home and thought she could take care of both of us.

I stayed at Betty's when I left the hospital, but after I thought on it awhile, I went to live with Willie Mae and Mack. Betty and her husband Lorrel had three small children to raise and it seemed easier for me to be with Willie Mae and Mack. After I moved in with Willie Mae, Betty moved over to Oakland. Once she moved there, she found another job. She hardly comes over here anymore, but we usually go over every weekend. I still do wood work in her garage.

I feel real close to Betty. I call her every morning at six o'clock so she can take her bath before she go to work. I call Betty every morning; not one morning, every morning. Sometimes she be asleep, but she always has to kiss me before she get off the phone and I have to kiss her. That's just how close we are. She thinks there's nobody in the world like me. We raised her from a baby. Every time I call her, she gonna kiss me before I hang up the phone. I still call her "Cat."

About three years ago we was up in Clear Lake. We had been playing cards one night. When all the people left, I told Mack and Willie Mae I was going to go and lay down and relax. I sat down in a chair. Next thing I know, Mack was holding me. I wondered what he's holding me for. He told me that Willie Mae was calling the ambulance. I knowed what had happened then. I had another heart attack. They took me to the nearby hospital and I stayed there a week.

I do all right now, but I can't go to the ball games anymore. I can't go up and down the steps. There's a lot of steps. That sure hurt me. But I enjoys baseball still, watching the games on television or listening on my radio. I keep my radio all the time so I can get the ball game when they're not on TV. It's not the same, but I still enjoys it.

In 1991, Coleman died when he was eighty-six years old. He had one stroke. Well, it's quite natural after he had the first stroke that he went to the doctor. But he wouldn't do like the doctor tell him. After he got all right, he didn't go to the doctor no more. He wouldn't even go for a check-up or nothing.

His wife was in one bed in one room, and he was in another. He had another stroke. He got out of the bed, and he laid on the floor there 'til the next morning. She found him on the floor. If she'd knowed, she could have gotten help. It would have been different.

Well, after he had that other stroke, he never got over it. It was so bad. He had to be fed through tubes in his nose. Coleman was still so mean, he'd just tear everything they fixed. He'd tear the entire thing out. He'd get it loose. He also got out of the bed, but he couldn't go nowhere after he got out of the bed. He wanna come home. He gonna go home.

He was so bad off, they had to bring him to a nursing home. When they came to take him out of the hospital to take him to the nursing home, he knew that they weren't carrying him home. He started raising sand at the hospital because he wanted to come home and he couldn't come home. That hurt him for a long time.

At the nursing home, they used a feeding tube. He raised so much sand about the feeding tube that I talked to his doctor. They cut a hole in his side to feed him through his side. That made it much better. But he was just so mean. He was mean to the nurses. He was mean to the doctors. When they put these things in his nose to get him to breathe, he wouldn't take them out, but they wouldn't stay in there. When he would move his head, the tubes would fall out. They weren't the right size or something.

We left to go to Texas to visit Mack's family. I told Willie Mae, "I'm going to trim Coleman's hair because he's not gonna live much longer." I was worried because the breathing tubes kept falling out. I trimmed his hair before we went on to Texas. The week after we got back, Coleman passed.

My brothers that grew lived long lives. Coleman was eighty-six when he died and so was Monk. Monk was living with George in Los Angeles when he died. George is eighty-seven.

George worked for Quaker Oats from the time he went to Los Angeles until he retired. He was a handy man and could fix anything. Sometimes they left him in the plant all by himself, if they needed him. He sure could fix things good. He learned himself how to do everything just by looking at other people. Don't care what he saw, just paid attention. He could do lots of things as far as machinery was concerned. Now, Coleman didn't take the time to look. He could cook anything, but he couldn't fix nothing.

I'm slowing down some, but I still do woodworking. I enjoys that. It keeps me going just something to do. I have woodworking tools at Betty's house in Oakland that I use whenever I go there. I gotta do something. I just can't do nothing. It got too hard to stand and work now, so I learned how to make things sitting down. I make things like knotted pine tables and stools. We have one at the house in Clearlake. I also built a little shed at the lake for to put a tub in there to wash greens on the outside without taking them in the house. I got a top over the shed so it can't rain in there.

I had a vegetable garden here at Willie Mae's that I loved to take care of. Willie Mae would like me to grow flowers, but I don't grow no flowers. I like to grow something to eat. I was always out there fooling around, doing something. I didn't plant this year though; it's too hard to do now. When I'm home now I watch TV—especially baseball.

The other thing I still do is cook. For New Year's I made gumbo and sweet potato pies. Willie Mae likes my peach cobblers. I make the crust good. I make the crust out of Crisco. I take that and I stir it up with flour and I can feel it 'til it get like I want it. And then I put Pet Milk in there and get it softened up and get it just like I want it. The Pet Milk makes it fluffy. It's a lot of work, but I like to do it.

Just Like My Daddy Started Me

Two years ago, Willie Mae and I went back down to Bunkie because I wanted to go back and look for the farm. I wanted to see the trees around where the house was, and the peach trees I helped plant with my daddy before he died. I helped him plant them trees. I just wanted to look at the place, see if it's still there, see if the trees and the house were still there.

I went with Willie Mae and Levi. We got mixed up and couldn't find our farm. Everything about the town was different. When I was a kid, you could see that church sitting on top of the hill, when you crossed the bridge. My mother is buried at that church. The church ain't there no more. When I crossed that bridge, it wasn't the same. When I crossed that bridge I ain't saw nothing that was the same. There are trees all around. I couldn't see where to go. I could see how to go around Bayou Boeuf, but not the side I want to go on. The side I could go on went to Cheneyville, and had a freeway going through there. There was no train tracks. That's what throw me off from finding the farm.

Sometime soon, I'll go back with Willie Mae, and take the time to find the farm and other places I remember. Willie Mae and I will take a train back to Louisiana. I don't like to fly. I only take trains. Once I find the train station in Bunkie, I can find the road that led to Bayou Boeuf. Just cross the bayou at the train station, then make a left turn and go right around the road to Daddy's farm. Just follow that road about two and half miles, right to that house. What confused me last time was I never got to the train station. I never got there. If I could find the train station, I could find my way.

Most of my old friends are gone, but I got a few good friends. Some of them younger than me and some older than me, they all gone. People at the sugar refinery and the sawmill quarters; all them people gone. All I played ball with in Louisiana, they all gone. Every last one of them. I don't know now anyone living that I played ball with. Young ones and old ones. They all gone. But I'm happy I lived to be this age. That's a blessing for me I got to be this old. I got something to be thankful for.

One of the only ones still around is Leon Diel. I knew at Leon in Bunkie. Leon lived right there in town and I've known him ever since he was a kid. I'm about ten years older than him. Now, he lives two blocks away from me. His wife, Inez, is from Meeker. She lived on a farm not far from me, and I knowed her when she was going to school in Meeker. With Leon and Noodnie, I got a little bit of Louisiana real close. They just love me, and I love them. I talk to him every day almost about baseball, about the Giants. He loves baseball and I do too.

This is a good year. The Giants are winning the Western Division this year. Dusty Baker, he should be the Manager of the Year. He should be, the way he brought 'em back. When they sold Matt Williams two years ago, got rid of him and took that money and got different players, in two years time, he got that club where they at now. He did a good job. A wonderful job.

One thing Dusty Baker still got to do is teach them how to bunt the ball. They gonna get them men on second, they gonna get them in scoring position. Baker, he won't do that. That's the name of the game, getting them in scoring position, cause you never know what might happen.

One of the nice things in my life now are family and friends. We got a big family. I got five generations alive—I got five great-great grandchildren. I just enjoy all of them. They all come round to see me. Always gonna see some of them.

I want my children and all of my grandchildren to know that the main thing is knowing how to treat people like you want to be treated. If you got a little more than that person, you don't think that you is better than that person, 'cause you are not. Be lovely to people. Talk to them like you want them to talk to you. I think about what my grandma told me. She say, 'If somebody throw a brick at you, you throw a piece of bread.' That's what the Bible say. I always did that. I always treat people like I want them to treat me. They do me bad, I throw a piece of bread at them. I ain't gonna do like they did me. That's why I been lucky all my life.

I come up like Daddy started me up. Stay out of trouble. Stay away from bad guys. That's when they get into trouble, when you go along with the bad guys. They gonna entice you to do this or do that. It's natural you go along with 'em. You go along with 'em, you gonna do something that they do. So when I run across those kind, I just leave them alone. That's just the way I live. My brothers stayed away from trouble, too.

It don't matter what other people do. That don't change me, make me do like they do. No, no, no. I won't go against how they raised me. You see people do people so bad and so forth. Lots of times you see on TV, how people were treated, and I read it and see it, and I think about myself, that I could not do something like that, you know. If I go around with people who talk all kind of bad talk, that don't change me. It didn't make me change and do what they do. No, no, no. That's just the way I grow up. I growed up just like my Daddy started me.

Don't hate nobody. Don't hate nobody. Somebody, like a friend of mine or something, he can do me something, and I think I never speak to him no more. But in a few of days, I done forgot about it. I speak to him. He don't need to speak unless he wants to. And I got along fine doing that. I got along a whole lot better than I would by trying to misuse people cause they been misusing me. That's the way I was raised. That's why I do that. The mad just goes away from me. Yeah, yeah.

I never had nobody tell me I can't do it. That's why I kept going. I kept learning, just by myself. No one but my father taught me anything. I don't know how I did it. I don't know myself, but I never let anything stop me. No one could tell me that I couldn't do it. I just kept going and learning. I know from way back what all I learn't just by listening at people talk. You learn a whole lot by just listening. You learn more than you would by talking.

Daddy and Mama had seven of us. They got along so well on the farm, they just forgot to send us to school. Just plain forgot to send us to school. If they had sent me to school, I would really have been something. Look what I did without going. If I had an education, I know I would have had money because I just figure out the things I would have did if I had gone to school. When I was working on the waterfront, if I just had went to the fifth grade, just the fifth grade, I could have been a walking boss. That's nothing but money; a walking boss make good money.

My family got more schooling than I did. Willie Mae finished school and so did her children. She raised three children, Betty and Leon, and Mack's son, Benny. Benny works at Stanford as a computer technician. Betty, works for Pacific Bell. Before that she worked for UPS. Sonny worked as a traffic control officer before he moved to Sacramento. All of them did pretty good.

Even though I was young when my Daddy died, I learned how to do things by my Daddy. I went everywhere he went. I was right there with him. I learned so much from following him just to see what all he do and how he make a living. He worked hard, and whatever he did, he did good. That's what counts. He didn't do something that wasn't no good. Just thinking about what he did kept me going when things were tough. How my Daddy raised me stayed with me. But I could have been there with them. We all would have been together, if they hadn't been killed.

Epilogue

෴

Beginning in the autumn of 1998, Mr. Wilson began having "spells." As he told it, "I blank out and then wake up real soon. One time I was at Trina's [his great granddaughter's home, in Stockton] and had a spell. They called 911 and an ambulance come for me. They took me to the hospital and I was just fine. When I was in the ambulance, they asked me questions like where was I. I told them I was at Trina Black's. They kept asking me questions. I answered them all."

Willie Mae had been in the front seat of the ambulance and laughed at the memory of the ride. Although her father had passed out for a few minutes, as soon as he awoke he was alert and asked her where his shirt was. Willie Mae told him that he was still wearing it. One of the paramedics asked why he was worrying about his shirt. When Willie Mae told him that her father always kept some money in his pocket, the paramedic said, "If he's worrying about his money, he'll be just fine." He was for awhile.

"When we got back to San Francisco, my doctor put a monitor on me to figure out what was wrong with my heart. One night, I'm sitting watching television and I hear a beep. I forgot what it was. Then a few minutes later, I hear another beep. I remembered and wrote down the times of the beeps and told the doctor the next morning. They scheduled me for a pacemaker the first of October.

"But before that, I had another spell. One day I was sitting at the kitchen table and had a spell. I hit my head on the window blinds and it woke me up. Right away I had another. Willie Mae and Trina were there."

When Mr. Wilson fell down the second time, Trina pressed on his chest the way her grandmother had taught her. Willie Mae called 911. Mr. Wilson was taken to the hospital and immediately scheduled for a pacemaker. The surgery was successful. "They figured out that what caused my heart problems was that I wasn't taking my thyroid medicine no more. My thyroid was taken out in 1971 and I got to take medicine. I ran out and never got more. Didn't think nothing about it. My new doctor traced back to the cause. I feel fine now. The doctor said it'll last ten years."

Shortly after Thanksgiving, Mr. Wilson developed pneumonia and was hospitalized twice. He spent December recuperating at home. I saw him just before I left for a vacation from which I would return on New Year's Eve. As he lay in a hospital bed, he spoke slowly and hesitantly, but firmly. He wished me a good vacation, and let me know he was looking forward to my return so we could continue our work. He seemed weak, but on the road to recovery.

After Christmas, his condition worsened and he went back into Kaiser hospital, where he stayed for a few days before he was transferred to another Kaiser facility. Betty and Willie Mae felt that he was not getting the kind of care he needed and arranged to have him transferred to St. Mary's Hospital. As his condition worsened, he kept his smile and good spirits. Willie Mae, Betty and Trina never left his bedside and were with him when he died on January 2, 1999, at 9:10 a.m. Betty called me later that day.

The day after Mr. Wilson died, I visited Willie Mae. We talked of her father's last days and her grief at losing him. She told me the times for the viewing and the funeral, saying she hoped I would be able to come. I assured her I would.

I had never been to a viewing before, and wasn't at all sure what was involved. When I asked friends, they told me that in some ways a viewing is like a wake, a gathering of family and friends honoring the deceased, who lies in an open casket. Alan came with me to the funeral home on Grove Street early in the evening. When we entered, we were greeted by a woman who directed us to the room where Mr. Wilson lay. I expected a crowd, or at least a small group, but there was no one else there other than Alan and me. While I was disappointed at not seeing Willie Mae and Betty, in many ways it was good for me to be alone with Mr. Wilson and my thoughts. As I looked at him lying in his coffin, he didn't look like the Mr. Wilson I knew. He wasn't smiling, and his eyes weren't twinkling. I was sorry I had been away during Mr. Wilson's last days. Although I had seen him just before I left, I would have liked to have seen him again before he died. I touched his hand, kissed him on the cheek, and then left.

Johnnie Wilson's funeral was held on January at the Macedonia Missionary Baptist Church, a church he had loved and attended since 1948. Alan and Sara, my oldest daughter, were unable to come, but Alexandra, my younger daughter, joined me. Forty-some members of his family mourned together with his many friends. A number of relatives and friends spoke about Mr. Wilson's life, each talking about his strength of character, his passion for baseball and most especially, his love for his family. His great-grandson, Yogi, recalled that he and his grandfather had gone to the Giant's opening games for seventeen years in a row. The tradition began in 1960 when Yogi was three years old and was taken to the opening game wearing a baseball uniform with Willie Mays' number on it. Yogi, now 42 years old, has continued the tradition begun by his great-grandfather and has been to the Giants' opening day every year since that day he first went with Mr. Wilson. Tracy, Mr. Wilson's great-grandson-in-law, who has been part of the family for nine years, spoke movingly of how much he learned from his great-grandfather-in-law. He described how in much the same way Mr. Wilson built fine pine tables, he had also built and strengthened everyone around him.

At one point during the funeral, Reverend Jimmie Hardaway, Jr. said that the family had requested a special song. Sister Edna Muse stood and beautifully sang "The Star Spangled Banner," which brought a number of us to tears. When she finished singing, Reverend Hardaway noted that in all his years of officiating at funerals, "The Star Spangled Banner" had never before been requested. I agree that it is an unusual song to be sung at a church, particularly during a funeral, but it is sung at the beginning of a baseball game. What better way for his family to honor Johnnie Wilson's passion.

AFTERWORD

❧

Much as when he lived in Louisiana, Mr. Wilson used his ingenuity when he decided to move, first to Galveston, and then to San Francisco, always looking for ways to earn more money and build a better life.

Unlike Louisiana, many of the neighborhoods in Galveston had been integrated since the eighteen hundreds. Blacks and whites frequently lived in the same block, though they didn't socialize. As in the rest of the South, however, religious and educational institutions were segregated; blacks were expected to sit in the back of the buses, and there was only a two-block stretch of the beach open to them.

In Galveston, Mr. Wilson expanded his skills and confidence in himself. His work at Hayden gave him a further sense of accomplishment, particularly when he taught himself how to operate the chair rig. "I let them know I was just as good as the white operator was." Other than this simple statement, Mr. Wilson never spoke directly about being a black man. I could often guess the race of the people he was talking about, but would ask for confirmation. Once I asked him what it had been like being a black man in Louisiana, as this was something he had never spoken about. He said that it hadn't been anything. "That's my race. I just don't feel anything. That's our race. There's nothing you can do about it, but just be your race." And that is what he did. He never denied that being a black man in Louisiana had been difficult, but he never let those difficulties hold him back. Quietly and patiently, he believed in himself and didn't care what others thought. Mr. Wilson found a way to be a man in the South without threatening the status quo and without being beholden.

After his death, I mentioned to Lorrel that Mr. Wilson had never spoken directly about racial issues with me, rather telling me of his struggles through his stories. He looked at me with a shy grin and quietly asked, "You mean Pop never told you that playing baseball was the only time a black man could shake a stick at a white man and not get hung?" No, he never told me that, but whether he was concerned about hurting my feelings or just not thinking of it, I'll never know.

Although Galveston was a good move for Mr. Wilson and his family, it wasn't the final answer. For that, he would move further west, to San Francisco. In 1944, when Mr. Wilson was planning to come to San Francisco, many others came as well. The city's population was growing rapidly. On June 25, 1941, President Roosevelt issued Executive Order 8802 affirming a policy of full participation in defense programs by all Americans, regardless of race, creed, color or national origin, and established the President's Committee on Fair Employment Practices. In combination with the labor shortage caused by the numbers of men being shipped overseas to fight in the war, Executive Order 8802 opened up new job opportunities for blacks, who moved from cities and rural areas in the South to find better jobs in the North.

As a major ship building area and port, the San Francisco Bay Area became the recipient of many people from the South, particularly from Texas, Louisiana and Arkansas. The black population of the Bay Area tripled in size between 1940 and 1944. In 1940, 4,846 blacks lived in San Francisco, 0.8% of the population. By 1950, the number had jumped to 43,460, 5.6% of the population.[xv]

Prior to the 1940's, blacks who migrated to San Francisco came primarily as individuals and lived throughout the city. When large groups began moving to the city in the 1940's, the combination of housing shortages, profit seekers, and racial discrimination limited the areas of the city open to these newcomers. The large influx of workers to the area was difficult for the growing city, as housing was very limited. The absorption of 27,000 blacks within a four year span proved even more of a challenge.[xvi]

Restrictive covenants, first developed to keep Chinese people in Chinatown, were extended to cover blacks. Ghettos were eventually created near the shipyards at Hunter's Point, where many blacks worked, and along Fillmore Street, in the Western Addition, an area in which Mr. Wilson bought his first set of flats. Forty percent of the dwelling units in the Western Addition had been converted from spacious homes into small apartments. Eighty-six thousand people lived in the 280 blocks of the Western Addition, an area of approximately 2-1/2 square miles. The black population in the area grew so rapidly that the neighborhood was soon referred to as a "colored district," although a survey completed in 1947 showed that only 26% of the area was black.[xvii]

As in Louisiana and Galveston, Mr. Wilson learned how to work the local system. He got a job on the waterfront with his new union book and worked hard in the ship's hold to build a secure life for himself and his family. He may or may not have known it before he moved to San Francisco, but the field of work he chose was propitious. The International Longshore and Warehouse Union (ILWU) had been integrated for almost ten years prior to Executive Order 8802. Although Johnnie Wilson never became wealthy, he was always able to provide financially for his family. And, despite the housing shortage, with time and effort he was able to find nice places to live. Buying a two-flat building gave him the ability both to rent to others and help his daughter, Willie Mae. Later, with the sale of his house on Belvedere, he was able to assist his granddaughter, Betty, and her family as well.

Mr. Wilson loved and accepted his brothers for who they were. Coleman may have "raised sand," but that never separated him from Mr. Wilson. When any relative needed a place to stay, there was always room. Lorrel came to stay with him after his surgery, as did his cousin, Phillip, who moved in with the Wilsons after he divorced his wife in L.A. Mr. Wilson passed on to later generations the importance of family that was so crucial to him.

Beyond bringing his family together, Mr. Wilson was able to provide them with a framework for their lives. Using the lessons he learned as a child from his father, he tried to instill in his family the ability to work hard, to treat others with kindness, to believe in themselves, and to share with each other. For the most part, he succeeded. His family is warm, caring and accepting.

In June of 1998, my husband and I were invited to Mr. Wilson's 95th birthday party in Stockton, California, a ninety-minute drive due east from San Francisco, where Trina and Tracy, Mr. Wilson's great-granddaughter and husband, live. Alan and I had long held plans to spend the weekend at a friend's house in Napa, also about an hour and a half from the city, but to the north. We decided to try to do both, since we didn't want to miss the birthday party. Mr. Wilson's party was set for early afternoon and we thought we'd be able to get back to Napa in time for a long-planned dinner with our friends.

It was a blazingly hot day when we left Napa. The drive was slow because of unexpected traffic. We were impatient because we wanted to be on time. This was the first time I was meeting most of the family, and the first time Alan was meeting any of them. We wanted to make a good impression.

Willie Mae had told us to come to a park near Trina's at 1:00 in the afternoon. We arrived at the park at about 1:15 to find that no one was there. While there were a few scattered people in the park, there was no sign of any party. Luckily, I had remembered to bring Trina's number. I called and she told us to come over to her house. The preparations for the party were still under way.

We found our way to her house. Tracy was there, as was Trina, for a few minutes. Mr. Wilson's brother, George, who lived at Trina's, was also there watching baseball in a room next to the kitchen. Tiffany, Mr. Wilson's great-great granddaughter, was working in the kitchen. There was no sign of Mr. Wilson or Willie Mae.

We introduced ourselves and tried to make ourselves useful while we waited for someone whom I knew to show up. Alan helped Tracy build a fence in the backyard to keep their dog from the garden. I helped Tiffany cook in the kitchen. I wasn't sure that she could quite figure out who I was, or why I was in the kitchen with her, but at my insistence, she gave me cooking assignments and we eventually chatted comfortably as we worked together. We got the corn and other fixings ready for the barbecue later that day.

Finally, at four o'clock we all headed over to the park where family and friends were gathering. We found Mr. Wilson sitting in the shade of some trees. I introduced Alan to him and turned around to find Willie Mae approaching with a younger woman who came over and hugged me— Betty. Of all Mr. Wilson's family members that I had wanted to meet, Betty was at the top of the list. His love for her was so palpable that I knew she'd be special. She was. Much as her mother and grandfather, Betty has a bright and warm smile, and I felt as if I had been reunited with an old friend.

Many things impressed Alan and me that day. Before the picnic I had known only Lorrel, Mr. Wilson and Willie Mae. Alan had known no one. Yet, the family welcomed us both warmly. We chatted with many of the older relatives and met most of the youngsters. It was especially wonderful to see Mr. Wilson sitting under a tree with his brother George, while their younger relatives brought them drink, food and company.

Unfortunately, we had to leave the party at 5:30, just as the barbecued food was ready, to return for the dinner in Napa. We didn't want to forego the ribs, so we took them to go. The drive back was quicker and more fun. There was less traffic. We had a lot to say about the party, and the car smelled of the delicious ribs we would enjoy the next day.

Beyond the welcome we felt, the warmth of the feelings family members expressed for each other, and especially for Mr. Wilson, was clear. He had rebuilt the family taken from him at an early age, and the love he was given as a very young child was shared with his descendents and returned to him in full. Being with five generations of this large extended family who seemed to enjoy each other, celebrating Mr. Wilson's birthday with them all, was worth the effort.

In the autumn of 1998, as I was leaving their house one day, Willie Mae said that they kept forgetting to tell me something. After almost two years of working together, I thought we had covered most everything. While we kept adding details, I couldn't fathom anything major that we had overlooked. When Willie Mae said, "Pop had another daughter with someone other than my mother," I was, to say the least, surprised. They wanted Hattie included in the story because she was part of the family. There was no time to talk that day, so we agreed to talk about it at our next session. I left feeling bewildered.

When I came the next week, Willie Mae told me about Hattie. Mr. Wilson didn't seem comfortable talking with me directly about Hattie, but wanted me to know about her and verified what Willie Mae told me. Willie Mae knew the basics of the story, but it was only when Hattie later came to visit her father, in December, 1998 while he was recuperating, that she told me the details of her story.

Her mother, Gertrude Robinson, briefly lived at Emil Jurett's farm, but left soon after she became pregnant. Gertrude died during childbirth and Hattie was raised first by her mother's cousins in Maryville, Louisiana, and then by her grandmother in Meeker. Only when she was grown did she learn for certain that Johnnie Wilson was her father. He, on the other hand, didn't know anything about her until she called him following Clara's death. Hattie was living in L.A. and found Mr. Wilson through his brother, George. Since that time they have kept in touch.

Mr. Wilson never really talked with me about Hattie, other than he accepted her as his daughter. While the circumstances of her birth may have bothered him, it did not mean that he would not accept her as his daughter, much as Monk was instantly accepted as his brother. The family that Mr. Wilson built was open and loving.

Much as for Mr. Wilson, family was of primary importance for my mother. Even as a child, as Mister Wilson did with his brothers, my mother worried about her three younger sisters. For almost ten years, the girls lived in an orphanage/boarding school in Vienna while my grandfather made his way to the United States to become a citizen, because my grandmother couldn't afford to care for her daughters.

There is virtually nothing that a family member could do that would have estranged them from my mother. While she might not have approved of nor understood an action, if they were family, they were family. For both sides of my extended family, she became the central figure. When my father and his siblings squabbled, as they often did, it was my mother who helped find a resolution. My mother never spoke of "raising sand," but the feeling was the same. Family came first, before any outsiders.

One of the ways both Mr. Wilson and my mother gave to family was by feeding them. Mr. Wilson first learned to cook from his brother, Coleman, when he joined him in San Francisco. Beginning by cooking on his radiator, his repertoire expanded when Clara joined him. By the time I met him, he had long been a skilled chef. Everything from Louisiana fish to gumbo and especially his peach cobbler and sweet potato pie were thoroughly enjoyed by family and friends. The day Mr. Wilson described his technique for making sweet potato pie, he gave me one to take home. After tasting his gift, my family urged me to ask him about other recipes in his repertoire hoping that as he described his techniques, he would give me other samples.

I don't know when my mother first began cooking, but by the time I was old enough to be aware, she was considered to be a wonderful cook and baker. I say "considered" because as a child I loved hamburgers, fries and pizza, not goulash and stuffed cabbage. This split between Hungarian food was most pronounced at Thanksgiving when one end of the dining room table was loaded with turkey, mashed potatoes and canned cranberry sauce, and the other with traditional Hungarian fare. Those of us born in the U.S. sat at one end, our elder relatives at the other, bemoaning the tastelessness of American food. I did love her baked goods, especially her kugelhauf (sweet yeast cake) and palascintas (crêpes with apricot jam).

Until 1999, my mother continued to live in the same small house where she had lived since 1946. In addition to the freezer that was part of her refrigerator, my mother had a free-standing freezer in the basement. Although she lived alone, both freezers were always full. She was always prepared for visitors, both in giving them a good meal when they arrived, and in sending another meal or two home with them.

Several years ago, when I was visiting my mother, she mused about her death. She said she didn't want a funeral; that there was no one to come. I disagreed with her, and reminded her that a few days earlier on Mother's Day, there had been more than twenty family members at her home. Some of my younger cousins had traveled from as far as Massachusetts and Maryland to be with her. I then added, "Tell you what, after whatever we do, we'll bring everyone home and eat what's in your freezer."

My mother's face glowed with joy. "I'd like that." And she would. Imagine being able to feed and care for family even after death. If I had asked, I expect that Mr. Wilson would have had a similar dream.

Susan and Johnnie, Stockton, California, 1998.

END NOTES

i   Spider webs have a chemical coating on the silk that includes fungicides and bacteri-cides. Covering a wound with a web helped stop bleeding and facilitated the healing. Fritz Vollrath, "Spider Webs and Silks," *Scientific American,* March, 1992: 74-75

ii   According to the 1910, US Census, Mr. Wilson's younger sister was named Lyan. There is no mention of an older sister named Maggie. It is unknown if she was away at the time of the census, or was a relative who came to live with the family after 1910 and was accepted as a "sister." Mr. Wilson was dead when the census information was collected and therefore could not solve the mystery.

iii   The 1910 US Census shows that Philip Wilson owned his farm in Rapides Parish.

iv   Corinne L. Saucier, *History of Avoyelles Parish, Louisiana* (Pellican Publishing Company, New Orleans, 1943), 261-262.

v   Saucier, 261-262.

vi   Saucier, 140.

vii   1910 United States Census.

viii   Leon F. Litwack, *Trouble in Mind* (Alfred A. Knopf, New York, 1998) 284.

ix   1910 United States Census.

x   1920 United States Census.

xi   Litwack, 41-42.

xii   Saucier, 97.

xiii   1920 United States Census.

xiv   Kaiser Permanente is a prepaid health care provider.

xv   Douglas Henry Daniels, *Pioneer Urbanites* (University of California Press, 1990), p. 165.

xvi   Marilynn S. Johnson, *The Second Goldrush- Oakland and the East Bay in World War II* (University of California Press, Berkeley, 1993) 2.

xvii   *Western Addition District Redevelopment Study,* November 1947, San Francisco City Planning Commission.

Acknowledgments

First and foremost, I am grateful to Susan Lowenberg for convincing her father to tell his story and to Bill Lowenberg, who, with his words, opened a new world to me.

Johnnie Wilson's story would not have been told was it not for the day Lorrel Anderson drove me to the airport in the Quicksilver Town Car. If Lorrel had not been driving and speaking so lovingly about his grandfather-in-law, this book would not have been. In addition to Mr. Wilson's openness for our adventure, the enthusiastic support and friendship of his daughter, Willie Mae Mackey, and granddaughter, Betty Anderson, greatly enriched both the texture of the story and my life.

A number of people helped me move beyond Mr. Wilson's personal story. Will Scott and Wendy Singer provided immeasurable guidance and support. Without the help of Betty Williams, the Bunkie librarian, and R. B. Smith, a long-time Rapides Parish resident, our trip to Louisiana would not have been so fruitful in helping me understand Mr. Wilson's early years. I am especially appreciative of Peter Rutkoff for his never-ending belief in my work and his ongoing wisdom.

I am most indebted to a number of people who helped me shape the book into what it is today. Margaret Kaufman reviewed an early version and gave me the confidence to keep going. David Lynn gave me excellent editing advice which both expanded and refined the work. Caroline Kassis helped me fine tune the manuscript. And thanks to Jerry Kelly, who took a manuscript and turned it into a book.

Special thanks are due to my husband, Alan, and daughters, Sara and Alexandra, for reading the text almost as often as I did and providing clear and loving guidance. I am also grateful for all of my dear friends who supported me with their love and inspired me to persevere until this book finally found a home.

Susan Gluck Rothenberg continues to
advance the art and practice of oral history.
(Photo courtesy of Tom Hauck.)

BIBLIOGRAPHY

1. Saucier, Corinne L. Saucier, M.A., *History of Avoyelles Parish, Louisiana.* Pelican Publishing Company, New Orleans, 1943 (1).

2. Gaiennie, Betty S., *Notes & Documents:* Sugarcane Retreats South.

3. LeCompte Culture, Recreation & Tourism Commission, *LeCompte: Plantation Town in Transition,* Baton Rouge, 1982.

4. Phillips, Ulrich Bonnell, *Life and Labor in the Old South,* Little, Brown, and Company, 1941.

5. Litwack, Leon F., *Trouble in Mind,* Alfred A. Knopf, New York 1998.

6. San Francisco City Planning Commission, "Western Addition District Redevelopment Study," November 1947.

7. Peterson, Robert, *Only the Ball Was White,* Oxford University Press, New York - Oxford, 1970.

8. Hair, William Ivy, *The Kingfish and His Realm,* Louisiana State University Press, Baton Rouge and London, 1991.

9. Ball, Edward, *Slaves in the Family,* Farrar, Straus and Giroux, New York, 1998.

10. Daniels, Douglas Henry, *Pioneer Urbanites: A Social and Cultural History of Black San Francisco,* University of California Press, 1990.

11. Miller, Ray, *Galveston,* Gulf Publishing Company.

12. Cartwright, Gary, *Galveston - A History of the Island,* Atheneum, New York, 1991.